If 'All the world's a stage', it's on fire.

A Sense of Global Warming

Do you have a sense that something's wrong?

Social-story-poems - Drawings - Pictures - Sculptures

General Design/Layout: Blue Light Series
Author: Martin Ray
Illustrator/Artist: Melanie Wichlein
Copyright: Blue Light Series
First Edition

Other books in the Blue Light Series
Computer Comfort – (A modern approach to computer use)
How To Run Better (2020)

Global Warming - Time-Stories
Global Warming - Social Story Poems
(Social commentaries on Global Warming Awareness)

Stories of Lala – Stories of Hope – Children's stories
Stories of Lala II – Creatures of the Forest
Stories of Lala III – Tell and Spell (2020)

General Sections

A personal introduction

Contents

Prologue
Chess or Checkmate
Chess

A Sense of Reality

Common Sense

Inner Sense

Sense of Humour

Senseless War

Sense of Sadness

Sense of Hope

Epilogue

A personal introduction

This is a collective work but as the writer of the words I'm responsible for their content; so I have decided to make the introduction personal. When you describe something as 'poetry', it's a very quick way to put people off from reading further, for poetry is often only personal and vaguely understandable to many others. These social-story-poems you will understand. They are about you. They are like parts of a jigsaw; as you read them you will put the pieces together. The stories, like a jigsaw, form a whole picture.

I call them story-poems because that's what they are; they're not just poems, and yet, they're not just stories. Many are both and they are all connected. They are about social justice and its lack in our Globally Warming World. They are about the causes and effects of inhuman and un-social policies inflicted by the powerful upon the majority of our human race. These days, we're called the 99%.

If you want to get a sense and feel for the whole book, read the two pieces on Chess; they're from our last book. They're appropriate. We've put them at the beginning; so you can read them on the internet without having to commit yourself to the whole book.

Both of these social-story-poems hit the subject from two different sides. In our last book we gave equal voice to the 99% and the 1%. This book is a little different, for it has to do with gaining a sense about something that you know - is wrong. And that, as an individual, there is little you can do. And yet, only you can do what little you can. You want improvement? – Join a movement.

The time to save our world runs out. I have kids; maybe you do as well, maybe not. But perhaps, on reading these words they will affect you in some way. I have no idea. But they are words and it is a book; and what is a book but a request to read. Our world seems to run like that: we make a request, we get a response; perhaps we've been making the wrong request?

I, like you, am limited in what I can do, but with social commentary story-poems, well, I can but try, combined with drawings and paintings that say a thousand words. We all need to be affected and not distracted from the reality of the moment. Where we're at, is one of the few real moments in human history where the clock ticks and time really counts.

To get the full benefit of these social commentaries, some of them should be spoken aloud. I won't tell you which ones, you'll work that out, I'm sure. If you do read them, you may feel both - rage and sorrow.

Some parts of this book may seem just like plain old doom and gloom, due mainly to not being the happiest of subjects. There is some humour. Although most of that may simply be gallows humour, but often, even that, can recognize and awaken in us something that sleeps. Speaking aloud may or may not cheer you up, but trying it will bring you many hours of amusement and mental dexterity.

Out of all the sense sections probably **Common Sense** is the big one - which could be divided up and subtitled **Social Sense** and **Common Goodness** for they all relate to each other. As to the other 'sense' sections, well, you'll get a sense of where we're coming from, or hopefully, where we could be going when you read them.

This is our third book in a Trilogy on Global Warming Awareness. Humanity is at a crossroads and there is only a choice of two possible futures that await us. Our first book is about this choice. In there are only two short stories, one is about the seeds of our sorrow, the policies of the 1%, and the other is about the seeds of our hope, us, the 99.

Contents

Prologue

CHESS or CHECKMATE ?

Controlling How Earth Shall Suffer

We win, you lose, our planet we will abuse. We know all the moves to make; after all, our lives are at stake. We have the most powerful pieces in control – we rule this planet whole. Sure, your pawns are spread all over the lands; but you have no powerful pieces at your command. We can see every move you make and we will burn you at the stake.

Chess is just maths at the end; and we know everything, we just pretend – our PR Goddess told us to play the game this way. Confuse the enemy, let them think they have a say. But our pieces are moving across the planet every day; we control the rules of the game, sacrifice a little here and there; the end result will be the same. We will win this game.

We work 24-7-365 and yes, we know the planet will burn alive, but it's a game in which we are stuck, it's not a game of chance or luck. We didn't realise at the beginning that this would be the end, but the rules of capitalism have been fixed, it's like superglue, we can't change our tricks. So we just enjoy the riches as we go, after all we want to be around to see the end of the show. It will be spectacularly warm at the end, our scientists have told us – we educate and pay them very well, so about their findings – yes, it's a truth they tell.

But this is not a game of chance. You say it's maths, yes, we know it's not romance, it's about survival - we found out first - you think we have no love, compassion or care, well, we care about our families, yours we can spare.

We know that most of you live in the mud and that your lives are full of war and despair, we also know that your life is not going anywhere. Our PR Goddess of control told us to let you think you had a chance to improve, but in reality we rule this game, we know your every move.

Mental and emotional manipulations are cool tools we've learned to use. Hope and a chance of change, we let you think it's in your range. We confuse you and we distract, it's a game we play, and we protect our back.

War, religion, economies, hate, insecurity and fear, we use all these things. We control and we steer. This is our ship, we're in charge and it will stay that way, you will never have a say. You think if you move your pawns across the board you can play? No chance. Your game is lost before it began; we control the life of the common man.

You were told to "Remember, remember…," but you forgot. Okay, we had a lot to do with that, we manipulate a lot. The reality is we cannot lose, we have a world to abuse, and we're not finished yet.

Chess, maths, or 'all the world's a stage,' call it anything you like, you can even rage - we don't care - the rules are fixed and we rule over you down there. It's embedded in your long-term education. For a while you were ruled by Kings and Queens but you were slowly coming to understand what that really means - class war. We just monopolised with a new face, we're your masters now - we rule this place: Someone has to, it might as well be us, we move the pawns in this play, we do it very well and we do it every day. Checkmate.

CHECKMATE

Controlling How Everyone Can Knowingly Mercilessly Attack The Earth

CHESS

Can Humanity Earth Save Somehow

Yes, we understand - for you, it's chess; we understand that for you, life is just a game, something to be won, to increase the power of the player and his name. And mostly we understand that you distract us with new toys, or simply despair. We know you manipulate and you fight for your control, you do it very well, but in a sense, you sold what some people would call your soul.

There is a common goodness that you have lost, it's a sadness that you don't feel and see, your actions are at a high cost; you're blind to this reality. You live in a hall of mirrors where you only see and feel what you project. You the powerful have been embedded to be this way, where you think you must rule and must have the say. Well yes, it's a normal weakness of man, where he thinks he must protect. It's a form of power that's for sure, but anyone can be this negative, you learn that as a child. There's a strange pleasure in a cruelty if it goes a little wild. To seek dominance and control can never leave you whole; it leaves a shadow, a darkness lying on the inner life of man.

It stops you from being a whole human capable of seeing and understanding the position of others, to put yourself in their place, to see or feel the suffering upon their face, the death and destruction and endless sorrow that your policies bring today and tomorrow. No, you have no power for this human capacity, you're weak, you've fallen down to the lower level of man, and you protect your position with all you can. The smallest child has more 'Being' than you the 'powerful man'.

To treat life as a game, that's such a shame. Life is more like a test and you fall down like all the rest - of your kind - you think you are the king and you lead the blind. You are simply a pawn of your lower self and you lead humanity towards this 'Endgame', and yes, in yourself, you are to blame, for not saying 'No'. This is not how it should go.

Being in charge and in power, you could have guided all humanity to a better end than this. You could have – had you been educated to lead

humankind. But it's no exaggeration to say, you are the blind, blinded by the attraction of power. You drenched a society in empty sadness; it's not wrong to say this is madness. Yes, we see you call this Chess; you think it's a game. No, that's a mistake, sadly. When organic life dies out, it's a Tragedy. No one wins in this game of control. All of our children die the warming death. With no food or water, no-one's the best. Only the beast in man will be released - at the end. Barbarism has no friends.

A Sense of Reality

To Empathize - is the Dream

It's difficult to empathize when you don't hear their cries. Our media sends pictures at the speed of light but the controllers hide the torture of their plight. Those in charge don't let you see the reality hit; it would be too much for your emotions, you wouldn't stand for it.

So a little bit of news breaks through – intellectual in the main, it doesn't affect you with emotional pain. Just enough to occupy your mind with thoughts, it cultivates and guides your attitudes to continue in your merry way: another disaster, another war, another day, golly, what are they now fighting for? 'Give them some freedom, and they will want what we have, 24-7-365 media…'

Refugees: don't let them travel here to come and live in our land; our ways they don't really understand. But of course they'll understand eventually they'll want to be like us; slow indoctrination always does the trick, after a while they don't feel homesick.

So, these are the thoughts and conclusions that run through our mind, it's like having only half a brain, we're really half blind – unable to sense and see the reality of life, death, suffering, and pain until it's in our face and comes closer to our door.

The reality of what governments do in our name, it's a pretense, an unholy shame. The horror of this unyielding shame is barred from our vision for we'd all hold them to blame. This they know to be true, that's why media, death, and destruction are controlled through and through.

To live the reality or live the dream

To live the reality or live the dream, well, it may depend on what media we've seen. When controllers of might manipulate our kids' thoughts with a few well-chosen forget-me-knots.

Just 20 years ago films that had such violence and classed as "Only 18" well, it's now common place for a 12 year old face, it's how they anesthetize the young of our race, by blasting Hell into their mind through the eyes on their face to make horror on the screen, something always to be seen.

Who is complacent in all of this? Who accepts to be part of this media blitz? Those common films become more violent with each passing year, destroying something that once was sacred and that we hold dear, our children. Fairy tales are now only told to the very young, plonked down in front of the T.V. for the media song to be sung. "But they're so educational." you can hear people say. For many, sadly, that's an attitude that's been manipulated that way.

We seal the fate of our kids as their first machine comes into their hands; we bring them into the modern age with such violence on every digital page. And it's something we've been told to buy; the modern media lie.

Sure, modern times come and we must change and adapt; these days, almost with every new app. But this is not the point, this is our modern life. The point, to be blunt, is we destroy the beauty of their soul – they become hardened as they grow. Something solidifies too early in their youth; we've bought their future with lies instead of truth.

Those who are older recognise that something is amiss, something's gone astray and it's happening day after day. Join the party, join the plot, its consumerism, it must be bought.

What do you think? Is it right that we destroy their mind with a new 3D toy? One that hides the truth of the real, one that disguises how we really feel. We bring them to the party of the shadows on the wall, where we lose the reality just before the fall.

With a generation or two of increasing planetary heat, we occupy the young, the poor, so they'll think it will be a treat. Who sells this lie and who's responsible for making the laws that feed this crap? They steal the souls of our young and feed them to an app.

When 99% of scientists say Global Warming is on its way, who and what are the guardians of the falseness of greed, of stupidity, who are the guardians of this false palace of pretention? They are the powerful 'controllers of might' and their protectors, those keepers of the fires that show the shadows on the wall - where the people are held in the invisible chains of complacency.

Invisible chains are hard to break, but we have a Globally Warming
world at stake with one generation left of chance to change. It's being kept
just out of our range. Barriers block our every path, 'controllers of might'
have a wrath but no power to comprehend the darkness that they send.

Sending the 99% of the world into a living hell
while they use their magic sentence
"Buy everything we sell".

'Buy everything we sell and you will be well;
we'll blast images into your mind, so you'll think you'll see,
even when you're blind. We are the real keepers of Plato's cave;
you'll live in our reality, but "remember remember", you, we can save.
Buy everything we sell and you will be well,
believe everything we say and life will be better one day.
Do what you're told and live in hope for change,
look at those shadows on the wall, they're almost in range.

That's your reality that you perceive;
we told you so, so that's what to believe;
your eyes are open, trust us, you're not asleep.'
Unfortunately, they stoke the fire that brings the Heat.

Pre-poem for TTIP

Some Humans Are Mostly Empty

'There's a lot of talk of the rules we make, people think their freedoms and lives are at stake. So sometimes we must quell this dissent with soothing words and let them think that what we do is well meant.

But as we gather here today, let's speak a truth that only between us we say. Let's make it all black and white, because generally we use confusion, after all we are the 'controllers of might', of power, of control, we deceive humankind whole, we have to, we're the keepers at the gate, we control the human fate.

We guide, we manipulate and destroy with multiple distractions and attractions. We have many methods we employ, and we must keep in control and must guide the way, for our planet's warming and it's warming every day.

If the public get to emotionally realise this and see how we deceive with all we do, then they will seize control, so we must keep them guessing and insecure down below. Our people are working in the dark and we must dampen in many ways this potential fire, from any spark.

Power, deceptively soft or openly hard, is in our hands; we control it all; this we understand. 'But let's be clear', about what we do, because remember – you work for us and we work for you.'

$\mathcal{T}$urning $\mathcal{T}$rust $\mathcal{I}$nto $\mathcal{P}$ower

"Let's turn trust into power; we'll privatize it and bring a shower – of despair and sorrow – like there's no tomorrow: for if we manage to turn trust into privatization, power will come to us without cessation.

There will be no barriers we cannot cross; the poor will realize we're the boss. Of course they know that well enough by now; exploitation is our game, gathering everything is our aim.

We've monopolized the free trade idea, money we've magnetized, it comes to us up here, and if we manage to continue in our ways everything will come to us till the end of days.

A manipulation of people through the ages, move the peasants into towns. Do it in stages, contain them in walls of 'home sweet home', trapped in the city's streets to roam. Barons of power with whip and chain - the city life - now man's domain.

Raise the living standard just enough that they won't complain when life is rough. Factories of employment where the face changes through the ages - dull down the free spirit of man and leave him with no enjoyment. Slowly turn the knife and twist until the peasants rage from exploitation of the masses of humankind. Man becomes the machine and to his higher life blind or blinded by mental manipulation inflicted upon generation after generation - right through till these times now. Where it's reached the highest art of all – public relations – propaganda controls it all.

"It's easy to control the mass of man, give them something to fear or hate and we'll control the keys of the gate. They will follow anything at the end; they'll even betray their best friend. Man has the beast in him; it just needs to be released.

Play on his mind with some tricks, give him a carrot or a stick; tell them that what we do is good for them. All the horror that we unleash upon the enemy they deserve. Tell them if we don't keep control they could lose their very soul.

Of course some do suspect, that we, the 'controllers of might' deceive them with lies and deceit. Some minds escape our net but that's a little treat; it helps to give the illusion of freedom, if we allow some descent, it lets the public think their taxes are well spent and that they have a choice – a voice. Of course we marginalize it, keep it off the main media that we control, let them think they're free, and let them have their bits and pieces of illusion. The end results for us will be the same conclusion. Remember, we control this game, we write the rules, the laws, our surveillance knows no bounds, anything 'they' do can be found. And if some voices do stir others into actions that we don't like, it's not a problem, we give them something else to worry about - that's the drink we spike.

Our people call it 'behavioural engineering'; we always know what it is the common man is fearing; and that, we manipulate to the highest degree, they are the blind and the 'befuddled silent herd', we are the ones who see.

We are the controllers enjoying oligarchy, we are in charge. We trained some to specialize in psychology, so we control the mind and into that we see; we control where the herd goes; they don't roam at large. We control the work or if there's any at all. We control how much they are paid or if they rise or fall. We control their housing and their quality of life. We control they spend a lot of money if they want a wife.

Our business plan is the biggest of all. We control all social life on earth. We control and manipulate them to want the latest car, toy or phone, we give them famous people to want to be like and never be alone. We manipulate from childhood and we embed it in their education and this is 24-7-365 from the moment they can talk every day they're alive. We have many pots that are cooking, many dishes on the go, we have something for everyone; this is our media show. We have the latest clothing, the new style of today, we change it several times a year; the poor public have absolutely no say.

Try this, buy this or die, live the consumer lie – think that it is progress and that you have your life in hand; well, you are the blind of our land, all you see is what we sell.

Play our game or you won't be well; behavioural engineering, controlling the mind, manipulating emotions or anything you find. We have led you to think this way and we do it continuously - every day. It's a bombardment on the 'sense of yourself'; we don't want psychological independence and common sense good health.

This is the world we live in; we control the keys and the gate, we don't want people free – in any state. They are our workers, this is our hive and we have our soldiers that keep us well protected and alive.

It's a class system that's manipulated all through time, we've just perfected the art, we think it's pretty fine. Sure, 'they' suffer down there below; but the real world isn't big enough for everyone to know. So we must control the herd – in our many ways – and leave them blind. They must follow us and have no independent mind.

If that were ever to happen, we'd lose what we have and chaos would roam. There's just not enough wealth for all these people to have a home. So we, our class, gather what we can, where we can, while we can.

And we don't have to worry, it's all under control. We keep 'them' all separate, fighting and struggling down below. If it gets to be a problem, we cause another war; it makes sense, it's good for business; we sell 'them' guns to kill each other. So you see how stupid 'they' are and we control this from afar.

We manipulate their religious beliefs, stir their emotions into hate; it's just another key for us into the gate of their mind. Always remember, we are the king - 'they' are the blind.

We make our populations fear what might come as blowback from the actions that we take. But they don't know we caused it and manipulated it to be so. It allows us to increase security, take freedoms away that helps us to control these peasants down below.

Some say our system is self-destructive at the end, maybe, maybe not. But it's capitalism, a consumer plot – once you're born, you're bought. And we will consume all we can, it's built into our system, it's the rules, it's how we today control the common man.

Remember, remember, we write these rules of the game and we change them as we go along, in that we have – no shame."

T T I P

Turning Trust Into Power

Turning Terrorism Into Profit

Topping The Intelligence Principle

The True Invading Principle

Truth Twisted Involving Paradoxes

The Threat Involving Populations

Trashing The Involvement Process

Taking Trust Internalizing Profit

Twist Those Ignorant People

Telling Tales Invading Populations

A Game of Control

Yes, we see that

A game of control, yes, we see that. We see you have control and we see in many ways you manipulate us whole. Your methods of distraction and attraction are many and cause the suffering that exists. What, you really think we are that blind and that we won't persist – to escape – to be free – to live in freedom and to learn how 'to be' human.

Humankind – a kind-human, this is something you do not feel or see. When you fight for top dollar or number one to be, when you destroy our world and our world will burn, then you must be the blind, if profit is only what you find – to be of value.

If you cannot empathize with the people who are in need, then you, the so-called 'leaders' should not lead. Leaders of humankind should not be to empathy or compassion blind.

It seems the system's fixed, but we know your tricks and one day the pendulum will swing – it always does – and you will fall just like us.

The problem is, our planet heats – and the time we have to slow down the speeding train we're on – does not repeat – does not extend – this is something humans cannot mend.

Sure, perhaps another hundred years of technological knowledge will come to pass. There will be some 'change of things', but nothing very important compared to what HEAT brings; this is just maths.

The 'Game of Life' was wrongly named, it's not a game, it's not chess. You lead our planet to this mess; it's simple at the end - in Barbarism – we have no friends: and that of course is where it will lead because you trashed our planet and let it bleed.

SHAME – yes, this you should feel, but don't, and all who work for you and manipulate all you do. Yes, it's embedded in this system; your workers have internalized their 'selfie' over human care, compassion and a world to share.

We know and understand deep inside, it was and is a cool trick, it's a carrot or a stick, and we know you will beat us down and with soft manipulative power or with a bullet leave a hole and bury us in the ground.

This is a tragedy, this we know. It's hard to struggle against your might, you are controllers of great power; but that type of power is a weakness – you're exploiting the soul of man – you are being-less leaders, to really be - you never can. You should not be leading this 'race' you call the 'common man'.

Humankind - a race of 'Beings' given knowledge, awareness and power to look after and care for all we see. We were meant to live in wonder about what we could really be.

This is the 'Age of Treason' where you have manipulated our powers of reason; where you have exploited all you can just to have power over the 'common man'. And you have led the people to be as common as you.

"Look after yourself, nothing else will do, ignore the old, the homeless, the unfed and those we kill or leave with no home or bed. Ignore the horrors that we bring, instead, go out and shop and buy something.

There is no alternative to this fate, our Goddess is called TINA and she doesn't wait, she has no compassion or care, and she's like us, not interested in you down there. Your fate is sealed, you cannot move; we stuck you in this deathly groove. And like a thought or habit of thinking stuck in your mind, it will be all you see or feel - you are the blind."

Well, to you the said above may well be true, but what an attitude to take when mankind is at stake, but not only, for all life on Earth will die because of heartless policies coming from you. From your towers in the sky - you look down on us, yes, we know. But because you're so high you don't see or feel anymore what's down below. No matter what you think – television is not a reality T.V. show.

We hit reality with every step we take; this is our reality and it never takes a break, like the evil of your policies that you apply. Because of that, our children die – and humankind at the end.

2 Minutes 2 Midnight

The nuclear clock has been moved to two minutes to midnight, it hasn't been so for thirty years. It's one of two possible endings for the human race, with the majority of beings living in poverty and sorrow. That's a helluva lot of tears. Two endings in a race through time – the other is Global Warming, neither will be fine.

The people of our world do not want nuclear war; repeat; we do not want nuclear weapons on the table. To have them as an option is an attitude that is mentally unstable. To use that as a threat comes from an attitude that can't be met, to blow a nation away, to obliterate a country of all life, mothers, daughters, fathers and sons, the old, the young and nothing will return – to live – a poisoned area in the body of mother earth.

"All options are on the table": there shouldn't even be a table for that form of horror – one of the mistakes of humankind. We are led by leaders who are blind, who increase the horror of all that humans find.

The nuclear choice – we never had a choice, the people never had a voice, we were never asked – to this horror on earth humans were masked – blinded by the powers that control the powers of might. It's they that have led us to this 2 Minutes 2 Midnight.

Look at your leaders in all your lands. Look at them when they talk. Are they in control? Are they stable? Are they able – to be emotionally mature? What dominates them deep inside, not what they show to the world, but what do they hide? In the darkness of their being, how stable are they? What are the options on their table of their inner sense?

Are they compassionate? Are they kind? Are they considerate or are they blind – to the better sides of being human? Does their control show on their face? Are they a good example of the human race? Would you want them to represent you to your God and say – "this is what we be" or do you think it's more appropriate to say – 'sorry – have pity on me'?

Are your leaders vain? Are they petty in where they live in their domain? Are they contorted in their face? Do you see the beauty of the human race? Not in body, but in spirit, in kindness and consideration, in empathy for others. Are these the qualities you see? For these are qualities that should be, a part of the real leaders of humankind, qualities of being. Are these the qualities we are seeing?

Probably not – just thought I'd ask. It's always good to question the mask of those that lead. Do we have leaders who are kind? Or do we have leaders who are 'players' for power and are emotionally blind?

'Player' implies those who play a game – that's not a quality in leaders – that's a shame. Looking older in a power suit does not mean emotionally mature. But yes, a 'Game', perhaps of 'Chess', with many moves or options to increase this Global Mess. To this end we've been led; are our leaders emotionally dead?

The first thing a real leader should do – to stable our world – is take the nuclear option off that fucking table.

LEADER: Leading Everyone And Destroying Earth Regularly

This is not a Game

This is not a game, but you call yourself a 'player', the un-normal to us, but normal to them: attitude of leaders who are not educated to lead.
These are businessmen who only seek profit and a planet to bleed.
To bleed dry of all sense of hope,
to leave misery where none can cope –
whether that be with austerity measures imposed upon the poor or a bullet or a bomb sent by a stronger, love from…
Us, the 'controllers of might', of power, of you
the 'common man'; and we are all the common man.

The commonality of being human or in a human just trying to be,
nothing special, just with compassion, care or empathy,
to see that commonality in each other, something to which leaders are blind.
Not all these days, there are some who break that role, this is true.

But when a leader talks of war or has policies of financial insecurity for the many and causes pain,
these are not people who should lead, these are businessmen.
They are 'Players' in their own 'Game'.

PLAYER: **P**eople **L**owering **A**ll **Y**our **E**xpectations **R**apidly

The Human Element - Free Trade

Money travels upwards in space, it goes against gravity as if in a race, it collects in a centre as if with a magnetic pull, it seems to follow a golden rule. This rule has such an invisible power that from the common people down below, money is something that they'll never know.

Trades and deals are made in secret, as if in the dark. The laws for the people all change; work is outsourced to other lands, the cheapest way of making things for corporate brands.

People lose their work, their pride, their power; and where the work goes, God only knows. The state of life for those forced to work for a dollar a day, millions of lives wasting away, slaved labour camps - life with low pay!

Companies can sue if governments try to subdue the power they exert, which just means governments can be sued if companies policies are reviewed, taking more money towards the top, the law of gravity, that cannot stop.

People die from these policies of control, people hunger and lose their soul, their very being ripped apart, company policy. It was THEFT from the start. It's people who make these laws, 'They' fight for their 'just' cause, to steal everything from the life of man, just because they can.

Controllers of might don't need to fight to stay in positions of power. One life at the top another below, it's like a magic mirror; you don't see the horror of the show. Destitution, Destruction and Death, Poverty, Hunger and Pain, all that and people complain! Well, all that and 'they' send wars with no name, make the poor suffer because they speak for common rights that they seek.

'Millions suffer and die every day, but they're allowed to breed. We need it that way, we feed them little at the end and we always have another war around the bend.

Wars always seem to destroy, but only for a while, for afterwards when the dust settles down, a new generation begins to grow. They buy our things to fix their land again, this we know. They will want employment and want to buy and try all we sell; and they will be the new cheap labour force, we use so well.

The devastations that come with war and the many deaths of horrendous pain, we don't feel it. That we never see, it's built into our system, how things have to be. It's the rules of the game; we, the people in control feel no shame. I have compassion for my dog or my cat, but for others in other lands, well, they can suffer that. We have a saying, we say it every day, 'Suffer the poor, they're in our way'.

T H E F T

The Human Element Free Trade

The Hope Everywhere Followed Trust

Trust Has Evaporated Following Truth

Tragedy Has Eventually Followed Terror

Turn Human Empathy From Truth

Turning Human Emotions From Tenderness

Tired Humans Eternally Feeling Trapped

Trapping Heat Earthbound Forging Tragedies

Try Hiding Everything From 'Them'

Try Heaven Earth's Fucking Trashed

A Planet in Need of Something

An epic would do as the ancients would 'a-shrew',
they'd write their poems sometimes without a break;
their history was not at stake.
No kings or queens to read about in these pages here (almost)
but power struggles. Oh yes, those things will be near,
for the main cause of our 'in your face' problem today lies in
our use of consumer capitalism in a neo-liberal sort of way.

This is just a little wake up remembering call,
to bring to the attention of one and all,
whose eyes may per chance come upon this book?
And through that take a second look,
into oneself and to the world outside
for there's something happening, from which we cannot hide.
For some, evidence floods the senses,
and heats and burns into the mind.

The storms come for many and wipe home and life away.
So yes, evidence floods the senses.
Due unfortunately to a massive constant blitz of lies
the faults were hidden from our eyes.

Much effort and money poured into their advertising skills laid bare.
Tobacco, oil and others from their deep
and never ending coffers of gold did seep.

Media advertisers started misleading
and to be selective in what they said
so a little bad weather came and left, many for dead, how sweet.
Confusing the public in the main
and taking money for things - there's much to blame.

If you worship the Goddess called PR
perhaps your inner moral compass has gone ajar.
If you've been helping to negate Global Warming,
then perhaps it may be helpful to simply - stop.

There are so many ways of saying it and so many ways of slaying it, but
here's a way that we shall try to help our Earth
before we betray it more and kill its health.

The thin circle of organic life that surrounds our Earth,
it extends from just below the ground to the stratosphere
and it contains all that we hold dear.
The hair trigger balance that sustains us
is being sent haywire and losing its ability to maintain us.

There are many things that could be said,
but it's fossil fuels in the main and this man-made bed.
Destruction will bring all people pains;
in the end no-one gains.

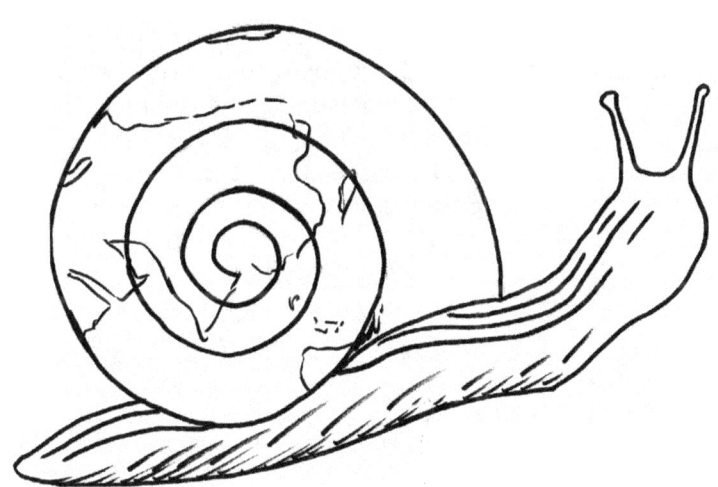

Our Candy Apple Planet

Take an apple; coat it in thick candy, those ones you buy at the fairground.
That's about the thickness of our atmosphere
and it holds all that we love dear.
From top to bottom about 190 kilometers: The troposphere,
Where we live, is life between 10 and 16 kilometers.
We and all of our companion beings live and die here;
it's not a lot of living space, but with incredible speed, heating up.

A window has been oiled (no real pun intended) and is closing fast.
Out of the many scenarios that have been forecast,
the end result was the same in every one.
It is simply a matter of the time past;
it seems to oil, or ourselves, we have been addicted.

The planet then goes under lock and key. It's a journey of no-return,
and no-one is able to truly predict where that leads to be.
But it's more likely that there will be no life on earth,
at least not what we recognise as livable for you or me.

On a planetary timescale, it seems that humanity exists just as an
extra, a late arrival that killed the party.
We were wild and did thrive, busy like bees in a global hive.
The coating on the apple is heating fast;
we have a little time, but it won't last.
Some people tell us 'It's all okay.'
Scientists say 'That's lies.
'Above a certain temperature,
everything dies.

A Call

With our sense of time things move slowly fine
for most of the world it doesn't seem that bad today.
Those people that experience all that we rhyme about and the information
in these pages that is there to be found out,
they know first-hand or suspect, that there's – something very wrong.
It's just as if it's kept behind a veil
for the truth sometimes can be very pale.
There are sometimes secret, silent, strong invested interests
at work in the back.
Those stem from many a source
that keeps us a little off track.

But if enough people raise their voice to be heard
we no longer will be the generation of the silent herd
that left our children deterred - and unable to cope,
and quite simply lost without hope,
with the effects that we are the cause of indeed, for in the last 25 years it's
mostly we who planted this destructive seed,
we now call Global Warming.

Sadly, it may not open that emotional door,
for being people; sometimes we do stay closed,
reading information that goes right through your head,
can be all too intellectual, for what you have read -
It often doesn't lie in your emotional bed.
Our society has unfortunately produced a world of 'Being-less' leaders. They
were not taught how to be, it seems the wrong people are the 'Guardians' of
our society.

That leads us to be where we are now: on a changing planet on the edge
of a praecipe, a 'small' gust of wind and over we go.
It will light that spark and turn into a flame and it will rage.
And anything that people do to encourage that flame
should bring them a holy shame,
for this was not done in humanity's real name.
'Homo-sapiens' means wise man.

Extreme *Information*

Deep water drilling, tar sands and fracking our world - a p a r t.
We lose fresh water supplies leading to privatization of water with many well
managed lies – an 'Art'.

Nitrogen pollution creates a dead zone in the ocean.
Warmer moister air means more destructive storms.
The new normal is now where it belongs.
Carbon Dioxide (CO_2) coming from coal, oil, natural gas, animals and you;
and the newer ways of extraction technologies did start.

The figures may change a little from year to year,
but in 2012 over 600 billion was spent in 'exploration seeking',
deep into our earth the companies were 'a-peeking',
to find more ways and places from which they can extract,
more of this 'crude-ness' just to keep their profits more exact.

Apparently the CO_2 acts like a blanket, keeping our little world warm by
trapping the sun's heat, creating our new norm.
Mostly it penetrates into our deep seas,
sadly, our oceans become warmer and the water expands.
Expanding water raises the level of the sea
and the sea creeps upon our land.
Its moister and warm air brings heavier rainfalls and drops it like buckets
upon you and me.

But there's also the problem of methane gas that's abound,
for that too brings the problem closer to us you see.
Trapped under ice and in the ground,
much is released, more still to be found
and when allowed to reach the air
there's no telling how bad that will fair.
We're told it's more potent than CO_2;
unfortunately there's much of it and on that scale not much to do.

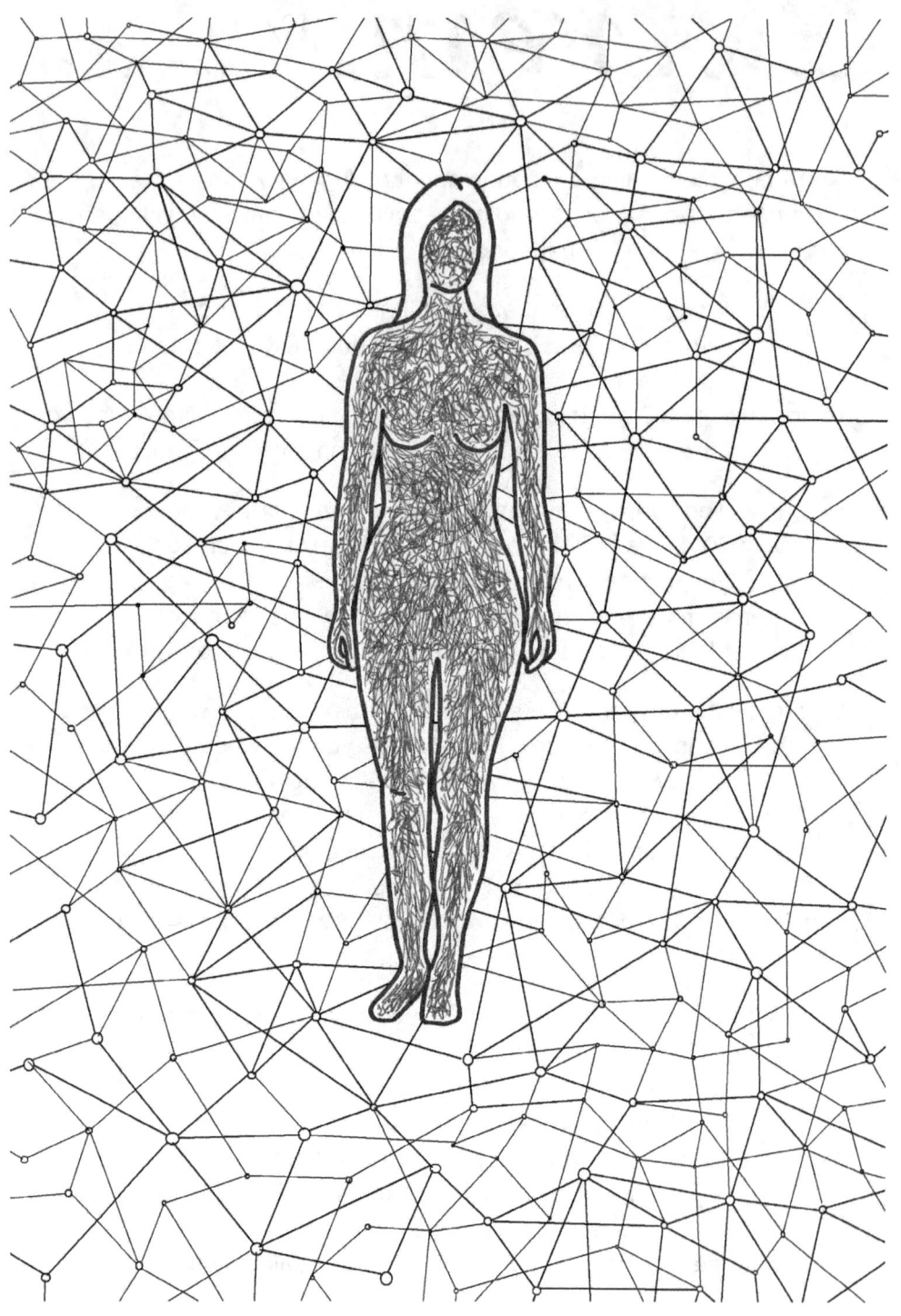

Prediction

Predictions from the World Bank, say 4 degrees we will tank
and for that we can thank our lucky stars,
for the IEA has a different say.
They're the International Energy Agency;
they think the number 4 is the conservative door.
For them it will be 6 degrees or more.
Life as we know it cannot exist when we step into that horrendous dream
and as strange as it may seem,
right now we haven't even reached one degree tonight.
It's said that 97% of Greenland ice is melting. Just out of curiosity; what
happens to the other three?

Tensegrity

Imagine a spider's web, in 3D;
the slightest touch stretches and changes all to be.
It adapts and keeps a balance; its changing is un-endless,
until the system is broken or damaged.
If there is no major trauma all the adjustments will be managed.
When CO_2 is in the air, it affects all systems connected by these invisible
threads, which is how they ought,
until the system is overwrought.

This integrated living web has been accelerated to
'comfortable capacity'.
The repercussions that must follow leaves nature in a hollow,
'stuck between the devil and the deep blue sea',
this is now the dilemma of humanity,
how to bring back a balance and how to be.

Wild Weather

As the water encroaches upon our lands,
we think it's pretty awful but we understand,
a little flooding will happen now and then.

But real projections will take their course regardless of what we think.
From the water of truth we all must eventually drink.
Flooding comes and overtakes the edge of our lands;
it's something we can't blockade with stone or sand.

Tsunamis come, that's not new, but it's their regularity and their
power that no-one living knew;
and if "all the world's a stage" and this is the 'climatic' show
all these storms are worldwide; you know that now you know.
It's just, unless it's in your face, you don't think of the human race.

Like a little ball of earth in space, from the stratosphere it rains down with
lightning all around,
increasing manifold in its sparkling show.
If it could be speeded up, well then we'd really know.

Hot spells and drying wells
but natural gas, fracking and oil still sells.
Nature doesn't take a break
when it's Mother Earth at stake; it needs to regulate
all the disaster at its gate.

The 'hottest' 10 years in human history within the last 15 of climate mystery,
a mystery for most but not to all.
Most scientists hear that call;
but a few others hear and dance to another tune.

Media ignorance or media manipulation,
how can they with their smiles tell us as they do,
that everything is fine and the weather's just a little a-shrew?

"It's a bit dramatic today".
"The sun has gone away".
"A bit more snow than usual".
"Wetter than normal,
but tomorrow will be the same" - Hotter than Hell.

Scenarios scene

There are many scenarios done for scale
that leaves our future rather pale.
There's a comparison that has been made
with projected CO_2 levels that's gone to upgrade.
936 ppm (parts per million by 2100 would lead to warming of 4-6 ^{0}C.

That alone stops much food to grow and working in the open air
would be regarded as a deadly dare.

In other words it's a no-no, but there are those that take issue there.
They think we step to a higher stair
and that these finding and projections
are conservative in their thought.

Due to complex amplifying feedback systems that eschew
pointing out the no small detail that the last time dear planet earth had such
high level of CO_2,
our little planet was 16 ^{0}C warmer than anything that humans knew.

And that the change we have coming at us now is happening faster than
anything we have a record for,
except perhaps the ones that the dinosaurs saw.
Now - that is just totally depressing news.
Do you have any other views?

Tell them and speak, start a debate,
you never know, it might not be too late.
You can bring it into people's minds to think
while you have a casual drink;
the theme increases your social potential.
Global Warming is it essential?

Effects are local for a while,
the sun shines more, that makes people smile.
How can a conscience be so small,
or a consciousness? It seems to hit a wall.

A Sense of Reality

The wall of manipulated thought,
there's no "Global Warming", it's been bought.
Some things do indicate very well what's at your gate,
you can tell. When companies think it's a good plan
and invest in vaccines for airborne diseases
that will travel to your land.
The bottom line 'Global Warming' that's just fine.

You can tell when they don't insure houses on the coast;
of that they do not boast. 'Dramatic weather, sorry, things are
changing just a tad; we adapt, don't be sad, we'll work out a package
deal', it's just the truth, that won't be real.
'Yes of course, we care how you feel;
this is just our present deal.'

Matrix of Systems

Desertification is under way, but only in some places we have to say.
Hot lands get hotter, wet lands get wetter,
but all in all it's not for the better.
It seems to be 9 systems in all at least;
that's what's written about our fall, interconnected one and all.

Experts in every field of knowledge tell us that soon we will leave our collage
of life and head out into the world at large.
So you better sell your house; your oceans are arising
your boat better be large, better still - buy a barge.

Connected like a living spider's web of tensegrity it pulls at every step we
tread, on a path leading to where we dread,
on a praecipe looking over the edge.
But politicians say, 'we'll be ok', they make a pledge,
they will try to do their best but their hands are tied.
With your pockets full, what can you buy in the land of nothing?

The wars will come for a while, maybe decades.
It seems pre-set to control the world. The 'net' is cast,
like insects jumping from Lilly pad to Lilly pad,
here and there, covering the whole planet
realizing or not that it's stagnating.
Beyond the world out of the pond, it does not seem to care,
about what goes on way down there?
It's a world itself; unfortunately, it's not got a 'bill of health'.

Of one thing we can be sure,
that those that have the money will feel a little more secure;
they can afford to buy a boat or a castle with a moat
or even bury underground; they may well be hidden there one hot day,
buried without a sound.

Later to be found, but after that period of time,
food will be scarce because of all the sunshine.
It seems to be according to study,
that acid in the oceans have arisen
and the last time it has been so high,
well, it's been 300 million years gone by.

Coral will lose its embodied life; symbiotic algae will have much strife; these
effects are sadly imminent and devastatingly permanent.

The release of carbon into our sea
is ten times faster than what it used to be,
before the last extinction - 55 million years ago - it's not fiction,
our oceans deoxygenate, our food chain will dissipate.

Global monitoring has been shown to 'sea'
unprotected marine ecosystems change,
affecting life on earth which means you and me.
It's now clear that we've sentenced to death life in our sea.

Open Heart

'I'm alright, Jack', what an attitude to pack

Imagine your heart taken outside, walking around, nowhere to hide; because
if you have children that's how you feel, nothing else is real.

These people, who are paid well to cause us pain, must have children in the
main. But what do you think they think about,
when nature's time is running out.

Global Warming means Global, every – body, worst scenario,
this century, everything progressively worse, not step for step,
but whack for whack, no turning back, heat attack,
tsunami, hurricanes, floods come and go, eventually to stay.
Desertification, food insecurity, for all – eventually every day,
not just for people of the poor, mass population and death
by one's own hand or others or governments in population control.
Border wars, the fleeing hordes of starving bodies,
no longer starved to death but droned out of existence.

It will be hard for media to say how three million terrorists were killed
trying to cross the border; it will have to have been an invasion for
food or the greater good,
for in the war of resources people become bolder.

Seemingly in place and preparation, borders walls are going up,
electrified all seeing and heat sensing eyes capture the terrifying
surprise – of death on the face of all, as to their data we can delete,
they won't be back and we've saved some meat.
Isn't death a terror 'treat'?

There's no way the rich will be that safe for long;
they've made a mistake, they got it wrong.
They followed their own rules and did not depart;
with evil actions they deleted their heart.
Too late to change capitalism, a dying deadly art, ART
'All-Rich-Together', but only the selected few,
something that we already knew.

Warm Times a' coming

The coldest summer months will be hotter
than the hottest of today.
Horrendous forest fires will consume all in their path;
there'll be no way to stop them burning 24/7 away.

People will need solar energised technology to survive,
for the extreme heat will burn everything alive.
At a minimum projection to mid-century, will be happening just as a by the
way - guaranteed every day.

If we can make social political progress,
we may slow down it a little on its way,
that's not guaranteed unfortunately,
but it's the only one window of opportunity.

The people in charge and causing the problem today,
quite simply will not be alive when these effects begin to thrive.
These people will be long gone dead and dust.
Must we place humanity's life in their greedy surveillance media and
corporate controlled capitalist crush? Is that a must?

The rich and powerful, have manipulated their power,
so now comes a thunderstorm, like we've never seen before;
it's not just a shower, and major species extinction means us.

It seems, for about 200 years we downloaded or uploaded into our
atmosphere, destructive carbon. But here's the catch, here's the
match that lights the candle that burns the flame;
the largest part of it was released in the last 25 years.

So, if you're reading this I'm sorry to say, you're a part to blame.
This is our unholy shame,
for we clearly were warned about 25 years ago that this was on the
way and now many of us feel it every day.

So, is there anything you feel you can do, is there anything you feel
you can say, even just to talk to people in your day,
to make it a topic that never goes away?

Bore your friends or interest them too, see what it is for them or you.
See how much people care, what they think deep in there – in their
heart – and they do – we really do.

It just needs to be kept in mind, that towards this devastating topic of Global
Warming, we cannot remain silent or blind.

Strange Weather, eh!

The blame is only ours when we are complacent, subdued, it
depends on how it's viewed. The companies that fight and struggle to
bring up oil from our planets depths,
those are where the moral human compass should point;
it should lead to their headquarters' steps.

For they have financed the media manipulated consciousness,
their 'PR' console the 'befuddled herd',
to keep them worrying about survival and next week's TV show,
then they won't struggle to be heard.

They continue to make the rules and regulations and keep the public
sheared like sheep and lambs heading for the slaughter;
it's as if these people never had a son or a daughter.

People don't really seem to understand conception of times.
And that a lifetime for a man is just a few days for nature.
The change is happening faster than we think or can perceive;
it's strange that people these things do not believe.

Melting Ice – "That's Nice"

Melting ice, sure 'ain't' nice; as the sun shines upon our protecting blanket of
white ice, it melts the barriers;
but we don't think twice. Oceans become 'bluer'.
Unfortunately, more acidic too;
what's left for me and you?

Sadly, the eco-systems take the toll
and on a downward path have begun to roll,
affecting the animals that live above and below – zero.
Oh, that disappearing white blanket of melting snow.

We watch "Happy feet" and the propaganda makes us feel good
about our-selves and it's a lie,
because when something's far from us, it can die.
And do we care? Not enough to try.

"Oh look, melting ice, that's nice."
Unfortunately the waters will rise and drown your city.
"Oh, but it looks so pretty."
Yes, it is and powerful and awesome too
and now there's nothing anyone can do.
The eco system reached its tipping point of balance.
We have a few years for our last chance
to minimize the worst effects of it
because burning oil is burning it.
The melting ice is just a part
of a matrix of a system, falling apart.

Desertification comes to some lands,
those dryer places where there's no birds left to hum.
Storms, hurricanes, tornadoes, torrential rains,
travel across sea and lands,
destroying all in their path, human folly, nature's wrath.
An adapting ecology in many and varied ways,
killing our planet of all that we need.
The animal kingdom disappears,
"We're one of them, aren't we, dear?"

As the oceans acidify, causing our fish life to die,
the food chain starts to fall apart;
causing feeding to be a dying art

Only some will survive in nature's changing path.
Seemingly it takes thousands of years to begin again,
to transform, back to what we know as the norm.
The planet heats, the seas warm.
The fish die, it's clear why -
It's a Global Warming.

The white ice on our planet reflects the sun's rays back into space
but there's some CO_2 in the air made by the human race:
that's me and you. Science lets us know these days,
that we've reached the peak of our ways.

We've climbed to the top of the fossil fuel methane mountain top.
Sure, we're still chucking it out, we can't stop,
due to our capitalist profit systems, the one they have ingrained into society
now and propaganda media systems maintain.

Its strength and its 'aqua-nuance' to the top 1% of humanity that is very rich
indeed, the largest corporations have their day and in every social political
system have a say.
Conscious manipulation step by step has been taken;
the 99% have been forsaken.

So called democratic countries turned into police states of control
as the corporate owned media massages all the information that reaches
those down below.

A class war, it is indeed, but it's the many headed ancient hydra that we
fight for our need.

Those combinations of corporate war and the military industrial media
complex, and the rules they bend to advance their end.
They use a means whereby that cause a shocking number to die.

The side effects of all they do is cause our planet to burn anew.
Our consciousness for others is rather small,
it's impossible to contain it all.
It's like we have a buffer that protects us all from the evil that we know and
see, that slowly kills our society - and humanity.

Decades ago it was the struggle to survive.
To fight for workers' rights to be alive,
These days due to publicity, we live a life of inane triviality.

Cultivated popcorn culture,

popcorn music, the popcorn vulture eats us to the core.
A society encouraged to live in debt
and to struggle through their life with needs unmet.
Wars kept far and distant from view.
T.V. controls what we thought we knew.

So, as we keep on gazing on the melting ice,
it gets more hits; that's nice.
At least it would be, if people were shocked to the core
and shared that info even more.
It's like we have a brain freeze with all this planet heating info stuff; nothing
seems to penetrate; we've been educated to be tough.
We're unable to really feel – immune to the life of shock and awe – failing to
see what is real.

Are we addicted to CAPITALISM?

Care And Participation Is Trashed Allowing Lonely Individuals Super Monopolies

A BLUE PLANET IN NEED

Many of the pictures of sculptures in this book are not solely about Global Warming but connected causes. Some reflect the land grabbers for mineral resources and seed and crop containment, thus controlling the access to food and supply. Others, the suicides of farmers in Asian countries, every 15 minutes, population control, media mis-information, war and global domination through force, fear and death: just some of the niceties inflicted upon a large part of our world's population.

Many people realize the need for a restructuring of values of our top-down society is a constant. The obvious and irrefutable connection of the capitalist way of life combined with the deadly policies of the 'Rulers of our Society', induce and strengthen in many ways - Global Warming.

That most of the world is under a profit system that is self-destructive, us with it, is obvious to many but not to the majority. Recognizing the danger of this has been negated and misdirected, thanks to well-oiled money influenced media manipulation.

Due to the way our society has been run we have raised the CO_2 levels beyond the limit of 350 ppm (parts per million), we are at 400 ppm and climbing. A level that has not occurred for over 300 million years, and which is the maximum level for what scientists regard as essential for the existence of human and animal life. We are at the tipping point of irreversible change, as in, the canoe is about to tip over, no going back.

Scientists from many fields regard it as an **"Imminent Global Crises"** *and inform us that if there were massive serious efforts in reduction of fossil fuels within the next 10 years and a transformation of energy resources to wind and solar, plus a few other important points,* we might just minimize some of the worst effects. This aim, some people have calculated, could be achieved by 2030 if the political and social wish and will was there.

It's predicted that in the near future our world population will expand by another two billion people. Over that same time frame, the majority will be orientated to living in cities which are becoming increasingly larger. The amount of new cities that are expected by the planners will seemingly match what we have already. These new cities, as yet unbuilt, will be made according to the energy systems and with the materials that we use now. That factor alone if left unattended to ties us into the continuation of fossil fuel use.

'In your face' - externalities

Sadly, the corporate controlled system that most of the world is under, ignores what are called 'externalities' such as 'Global Warming' and having a policy system that is self-destructive to our environment. Deep down everybody knows this. The public was informed 20 years ago; the effects have now escalated beyond all predictions, and are rapidly increasing, becoming as they say, 'in your face'.

At a certain level the effects start to lock in with other planetary systems that automatically speed up the process of Global Warming and Climate Change. Dramatic weather patterns have increased in the last few years sequentially, in such ways as many countries having their hottest years ever, each year breaking new records. The 18 hottest years in human history, were in the last 20 years.

In other places, there's devastating droughts and yet, the rising seas have become more acidic, which means killing off a large part of the food chain, also extreme heavy rains and floods in many areas.

I know, it sounds like the 'Weatherman from Hell', doesn't it, but there's no fun way to tell someone they're dying. Or in our case what do you say to someone whose house is on fire and they're not looking at it, even refusing to believe that it could be on fire? Do you turn them gently around and say, look, see for yourself? What do you say when they reply, "na that's not a fire."?

Melting ice has devastating effects, not only for the animals at the top of our world but eventually contributing to rising sea levels. The top of our ice world is almost gone. What was once a white reflective protective blanket to send the sun's rays back into space is now fast becoming a heat absorbing blue ocean; the south pole will follow. In other places of the world, record melting glaciers are melting which will deprive people of water and food sources for survival, increasing storms, tornadoes, lighting strikes etc. All of these effects will have other often unpredictable consequences.

Rising temperatures in many countries will increase the airborne travel of diseases, just one outcome of many predicted possibilities. Sadly, we remain misinformed on this subject, because of a fossil fuel and energy industry and, strangely enough, the tobacco industry in conjunction with a corporate owned media, which has and continues to finance, confuse and befuddle the public, rather than informing us of our increasing disaster zone coming planet.

Many of the rich controllers of policy and power continue to minimize the severity of the situation; they are, unfortunately, concerned with world domination and the 'profits' system rather than world survival, highlighting the short term thinking capacity of humans. The general public has been distracted and educated away from the reality of these life affecting issues, into a world of inane trivial pursuits, latest gadgets, TV. pop stars, holidays, candy floss culture, much that's superficial and nothing of substance for survival or even living. Or on the other side of the fence: people are occupied with daily survival, finding work, food, a place to sleep, the already poor being attacked from governments' enforced austerity measures in many lands.

A 'Corporate controlled media and connected military industrial complex' maintains 'the herd' in a state of bewildered panic. When people are busy worrying about where the next meal is coming from or who will knock on their door at night, they will have neither time nor interest or energy for action to help in saving the only planet that we can live on. That makes it a corporate controlled class and race war, in which 'they' are winning.

Human and many other forms of life cannot survive on a planet that's predicted to have a temperature rise between 4 and 6 degrees and rising more; it's simply not possible. At that level, most of nature burns. It then becomes a different planet. We are the last generation that can help; that's a reality and a responsibility that our children will see and feel, the effects of, us, turning our back on the problem, which is strongly connected to the problem of people in power, ignoring the effects of their pattern of behavior for short term profit. It sure sounds like an addiction problem, doesn't it?

CAPITALISM

Care And Participation Is Trashed Allowing Lonely Individuals Super Monopolies

Controlling All people Intentionally Trashing All Life Involving Some Morality

Cashing And privatizing Intelligent Thought About Liberty - Individuality - Socialism - Mankind

Controlling All Possibilities Involving The Advancement Lost In Social Modernization

Capturing All People Internally Through Attraction Lost In Social Media

Can All People Internalize This Attack Level Involving Social Mankind

Control All People - Individuals That Are Lost In Some Manner

Controlling All People Intentionally Trashing All Love Involving Saving Mankind

Controlling All Power Involving Transformation And Limiting Intelligent Social Modernization

Controlling All participants In Transforming All Levels Involving Social Monopolies

COMMON SENSE

A wall: like many other reminding walls of sadness, destruction and decay – of life – inner and outer – captured moments, ´Frozen in living time´ passed away.

Walls of Lies

Walls of truth, walls of lies, that just depends on what you surmise. Walls to hide behind, walls to protect, what is it that you suspect? That the writing is on the wall? All walls are temporary and all walls can fall.

Walls of brick and mortar or slabs of metal plate, covered in barbarous wire; it's a long way to find a gate, walls, too high to climb or electrified. Walls where people live on one side and on the other, died.

Of course we all die in the end but the question is on how did you live, my friend? Were you kind and compassionate to all your fellow beings or just the ones that you only enjoyed seeing? Did you feed the dragon that prevails in all? Or did you struggle to live the life before the wall of your being.

What was it you were seeing when you leaned upon the wall of being?

The Mother of all Europe

She struggles against the rage; they rage because she dares to speak, they rage because she does not want to be weak. All Europe had fed off her through times past, they benefited and still do – and now she's shredded at last. Our modern leaders seem to have no respect of memories of history, there's none to detect. It's business they say, 'Austerity works best this way. You will bleed your population until they're dry. You will rip their social net apart and they will die. We don't care, we're in control. It's a game to us, this you know. We will take any action that wins the game; and no, we have no shame.'

W*hen* P*ublic* D*issent*

It's a sad state, any state, that doesn't allow its people to debate about the policies of control and to stop a population from complaining whole. When public dissent is barred from intent, what do the rich and powerful have in mind? To what is it that we, the people should be blind? In almost every land protests are now banned or tied up into a matrix of extra rules and laws that to protest gives us no cause.

When public dissent has no legal voice, then the powerful 'controllers of might' leave the people with no choice. This act with pen and ink is violent at its base, sure, it's said with a serious face, but that's just a mask that hides the real intent, for these rules are held in place with guns and contempt, with water cannons, and sound blasters, with eardrums smashed, the people trashed, soaked with water or blood. The rules are made to hide their bloody hands and the plain fact that they rule our bloody lands.

They pretend it's for our betterment. Everybody knows the system is fixed and they 'occupy' us with their tricks. There's no soul, no compassion, no feeling in what they do, they are rich and powerful, this we know. But what about you who work for them? Sure, it's understandable; you need money, work, a life, to feed the kids, the husband, the wife. Society must continue, this is true, but when public dissent against policy is quelled, gagged, then they wrap us in a body bag.
And yes, there are many of us all; they don't mind if we fall.

We have a planet that we are losing because those in power and those that work for them are abusing their position. Our society will fall for this, while they occupy our kids with 'media bliss'.

Take a 'selfie', show the world you're here, you're real,
but it won't show you – or how you really feel.
Still, it will occupy you in the main, public dissent,
'Na, that's a fool's game'.

They can see you everywhere. You can't even cover your face in a crowd even that is not allowed. "Tag the public; we will know wherever you go.
Dissent from us if you dare,
we can find you anywhere.
Your phones are fixed, now it's real with GPS; we can you feel.

This is just the beginning; our technology will improve. We will hold you in the groove, and we'll embed it in your ID card and you'll have to carry it everywhere or from everywhere you'll be barred. There is no life without your personal chip. Fuck it; we'll embed it in your lip."

When Public Dissent – we whip them to repent: they think they can have a revolution and that's a happy trip; we'll leave them beaten and WPD – of this there is no debate; you don't get through our gate. There's a storm coming and you'd better hide, this is our bus and we enjoy the ride. We are the Kings of Capitalism, we rule, and yes, we are the cruel.

'Nothing Too Much' (I)

It often seems, it's no longer possible to descent
and free our-selves from a political tyrant.
Those who struggle to bring change, have a problem in their range.
We live in a world where consumption has been our crutch but manipulated
in 'strange ways'
and now many feel what isn't real and with whom it is that we deal.

The ancient Delphic temples had a saying about inner wealth
'Know thy-self'; it's said so much it's lost its meaning
rarely said with real feeling.

There was another, mostly forgotten now, but it was there anyhow,
as an equal to the other.
It was placed to bring a balance to the human race,
'Nothing too much'.

Consumer capitalism has led the way to heating up our planet
now, every day. We have a spit of turning flesh,
sadly; we're the ones on the mesh.
Trapped on a burning planet we have no choice,
if we don't act soon, we'll have no voice,
our life will become one of overheat, overkill.

We've been media manipulated and lost our will;
for that to transform a struggle must be born,
in which all parties must take their place
and join up humans in a race
to one voice one cause,
to become loud enough for the world to hear,
to fight the heat and darkness that draws near.
And dark it is indeed, species extinction through greed.

Carbon Hits, every day affecting everything systematically,
starting a reaction in an ecological chain,
producing the cascade effect on a planetary plane.

A civil peaceful resistance must precipitate a slowing down of climate
change, needing people to join in to that one world one cause.
We need civil peaceful disobedience to change our laws,
to encourage people to open their eyes and see that 'disgrace' of our
leaders and how they be.

It's a civil disgrace long in the making, leading to our protective atmosphere
now breaking.
People that take money from the fossil fuel industry
should be looked on as committing a crime
against their fellow humanity.

With companies reaching 'impeaching' profits and executives pulling
in world barrier breaking bonuses at the top,
it's hard to see how it could ever stop.
But leading and in charge is not where 'Beingless leaders' should really be,
not when we have a starving and burning up humanity,
from floods to droughts, heat waves to blizzards, acidifying oceans and
rising seas, this is our world.

It's a *Planetary Emergency*; it's the tipping point, the point of no return,
over the edge and the planet does burn.
One generation left to go, after that, it's a disaster show.
No longer 'Life - the Hollywood movie', for science tells us species extinction
is 1,000 times faster than normally…Now

This is now the 6th extinction, which includes you and me and our kids,
the last was 65 million years ago,
back when the dinosaurs ruled the day,
perhaps they'll come back in a sweet old fashioned sort of way.

The Poor

In all countries of the world today it's austerity measures that guide this play, this play of life where we live and die. It's mostly the poor, the old, the young; it could be you or I.

In some lands racism rules the day, in one way or another there's a lot to say. Do you get the feeling it's been manipulated to be that way, to make you fear a minority?
That may even be in the majority or not.

Young mums with kids tossed into the street, what type of life these kids meet? Many struggle to put food on the table, if they have a house; because for many, now, today, even that's not stable.
In lands that are poorer than the west,
their struggle to survive puts their very life to the test.

The rich and powerful in charge of policy have no compassion for those that suffer the evil that they do. Droned to death from the sky from some piece of metal flying by, not even a person in there does sit, just a boy sitting somewhere working a computer and presses a button, called 'hit'.

All for what, for access to what's buried in their lands.
We bomb and kill them so they'll understand,
that we in the western world really need all that stuff,
otherwise our life will get a little rough,
rougher than how it is today, as austerity rages everyone out of pay.

With not enough food in the mouth of our kids, we, the very poor, are distracted and attracted to levels of self-interested survival.
In these days, media manipulation knows no rival.

Who are these people in control and yes, it is people - this we know, who run the biggest businesses of our day, and leave a population of a planet with nothing to say about how life on earth should be.
These are people with no compassion for others, no empathy, towards the poor, struggling and dying.

In a world warming out of control with a 15 years possible chance of change,
our window of opportunity slips out of range.
We as a species lost our way; it's simply not right that the rich get richer
every day. That's something everybody knows and understands, but now
the system is locked in almost all lands.
A system leading to global destruction, but before the planet fries us, all it
will be is civilization collapse and barbarism -
it shouldn't surprise us.

There are many normal people out there in the world today that have a
conscience and something smart to say, about our world and the changes
we need to make.
I t's not simply about the 'let them eat cake' mentality of the rich.

A place in time will come where a revolution makes them succumb but by
then it will be too late for most humans at death's gate. Deaths in their
millions and then in their billions, as all systems fall apart! Daily survival is
the art, until the planet heats just that little more, that's where humans don't
get through that door.

So the rich get richer every day
as politicians pretend people have a say.

People who are mentally ill are beaten and chained for a thrill.
The rich and those who work for them tell us how we should live.
The country is a household economy, we should all give.
When a lot of our money is spent on war and death and organized in such a
way that we don't tax the rich,
then the rich get richer every day; class war again, it never left.

We see the poor and homeless in the street,
the untouchables of our society that we don't want to meet,
and we fear that end we may one day have too,
when no-one wants anything to do with you.
What a fate for a human being, what a fate we fear to see,
what a fate for the child in you or me.

All those people were kids once,
full of wonder and expectations of life,
led eventually by a society into a horror of existence of strife.
The poor, the homeless, that's not a life.

Compassion had to take a walk
the rich and powerful took control and told us how to talk.
Media manipulates how we think, from water of untruth we drink.
They're clever, smart with lots of tools of control.
Keep the poor uneducated, keep them a fool, distract us with toys, make lots
of noise, then we won't react to what they do,
as they trash and burn the planet through.

Punishing the Poor

To punish the poor for being poor: to keep the working class working, to put
people on the street, what a horrendous fate to meet!
To sleep in a doorway or in a box, no water to bathe or even drink, what is it
that the rich and powerful think?
Obviously not about the poor.
Desperation in the street, young or old sell their bodies to make ends meet,
young mothers lose their kids into government care,
if they can't house them somewhere.
Family history lost because the government and the rich don't care.

They care about your vote, but even then don't care if you don't,
they have the power anyway, they just pretend to give you a say.
It looks good on T.V. all those so called freedoms of speech that you see.
Where's the freedom in every call you make being recorded, where's the
freedom in every email being read. Where's the freedom when they record
you everywhere you go; it seems you're only free when you're dead.

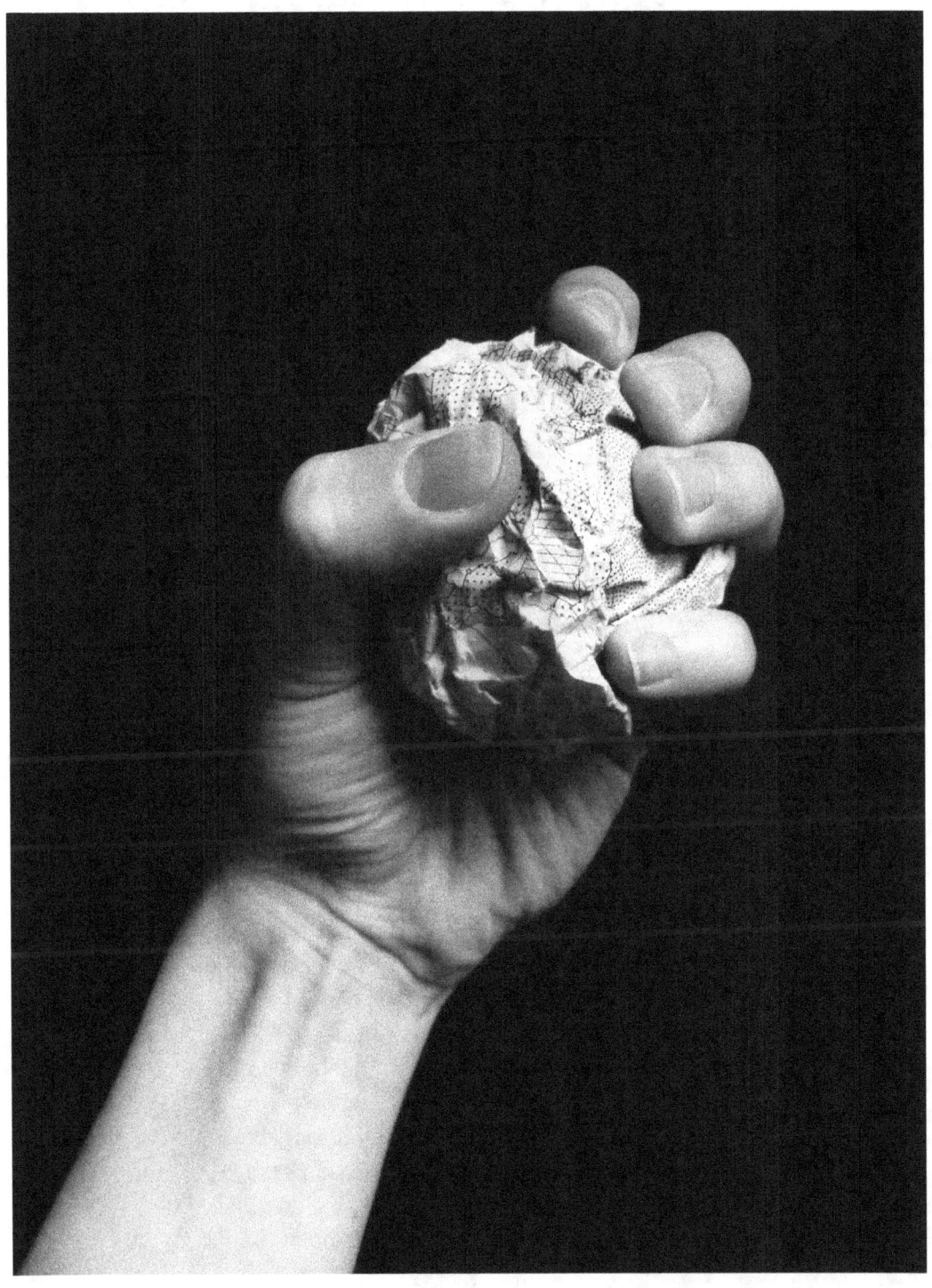

Cat-Food and the Heat Death

Everybody knows we fail as a race; it's all around us in our face.
We leave people in the street to die, an untouchable going by.
Governments in the pay of the rich elite of the world
create wars of domination and plunder.
Many don't believe in a God, is it any wonder?
Born onto a planet of pain to live, to die, what's to gain?
15 minutes of fame? Sure, for many that is an aim.
But what does that satisfy
except there's something in someone wanting to live that lie?

As we all know, most real things cannot be bought;
love and real friendship comes; they're not sought.
Ancient writers say that what we are attracts what we get -
and become. There are people that are happy with that,
but only some. What do we attract as a human race?
Well, obviously destruction is in our face;
on a planetary level it's really no time at all,
it's almost nothing from the beginning till the fall.
Is it possible to make a change; does that lie within our range?
Of possibilities there are many,
there are so many options on that table,
ideas are sown everywhere, but it seems that our level of being is not able,
to grasp – to hold – to help – to grow – for humanity, compassion to sow.

Of course those in power themselves protect
and any ideas against themselves they do reject.
They'll stitch us up in their net,
they treat the 99 like their house pet,
some bread and water, some kept alive,
if you're old and poor, cat-food should help you thrive.
It's a disgrace thrown in their face.
The poor they don't call the human race.
"We rule this world of plenty and all it contains,
you the poor will suffer all the pains."

See-Through

Rubble falls around our feet; it's a death only the poor meet,
having to move from place to place,
sleep under plastic - the poor of the human race.
Food banks supply our daily needs,
oh, how the rich make us bleed.

The laws are fixed to the society down:
'Clean up the poor, they lie around.
They get in our way and spoil our day, for that they will pay.
Put them in prison, lock them up tight,
the government will pay to keep them day and night.
We'll need more prisons built on time;
it's big business and it's fine.

The future's getting warmer, soon they will see.
We kept them ignorant as long as could be.
But now they join ranks and together start to rage,
they protest way too much and too loud,
no longer can we our intentions cover in a shroud.

They can see through all our actions now;
we'll need prisons the sizes of towns where they can live and slave away,
till the end of earth days. Society now will change for good.
No more will we hide behind and in the dark,
we'll be upfront, we own the park.

The world's our oyster and we shall it eat,
we swallowed the pearl it was our treat.
The little people die their little deaths,
after slaving through life.
But we have a need, we need them to breed.
Keep them in chains and only give them strife,
for they are the poor and they should always be in need.'

You Lose - Poor You

Children - taken from mums and dads - families torn apart -
austerity measures, the government's art.
The poor are made to pay for the banks'
and the power-maker's policy,
a policy of corruption and deceit.
'Put the poor on the street.
Take their house and board it up, wait a while,
drink champagne from a cup, a little time will go by
and we can sell it with a lie.
It is business; it has to be,
oh, how we love austerity.'

Politicians only have a few roles fixed for the camera to see,
sad actors on a stage,
they should be ashamed of their wage,
and yes, high it is indeed,
a system fixed to keep the poor in need
They say, 'look forward and don't look back.'
Well, look forward to the heat death, it's on the attack.

Do we have Real Leaders?

Hell on Earth

We have leaders who only lead us to war,
to a war of bullets and bombs or to wars of austerity.
In any land, you can take your pick,
these 'Being-less' leaders will leave you sick.
Shouldn't leaders really lead
and not companies the public money feed?

Shouldn't leaders try to avoid war at all cost?
Leaders should not allow wars to be privatised,
nor very little else for that matter.
Health or prisons or anywhere else where they our money scatter.
Where are "leaders" leading us there,
except into a trap of public despair?

Now these are people and this is true,
it is people that lead us here, into this Hell on Earth.
As politicians play their games they leave the people in burning flames,
whether from a bullet or a bomb, or a financial trick, all to keep the poor
where they belong.

Barbaric behaviour from those who lead us into Hell on Earth,
they create and uphold their rules and laws,
so they and their friends stay free for their cause.

One justice for the poor, one justice for the rich,
these are leaders only in name.
They are the leaders that lead our world into Hell;
and are the ones to blame.
Perhaps they have no courage to lead in humanity's true name.
None the less for where they lead us,
we will bleed and they are to blame.

After all, part of the manipulation was to convince us we live in a 'blame
culture'. So who are to blame for where we are
and where we're going?

It's those whom we have elected,
but many tricks they work in the dark undetected.
They have surveillance and control,
so the 99% of humanity will never be whole.
They have food and so they should,
for one day they'll run out of crude.

Wars of austerity on the people, wars of domination, causing suffering and
keeping them mute, financial wars like games of chess,
only leaves the poor in a mess.
The rich they will recover anyway;
the poor, well, some take their own life every-day.

Leaders should be ashamed
if they take pride in their position and name,
operating only from their mind, their emotions took a walk,
leaving them blind.
Blind in feeling; to lead us down a path
where it will take all our kids to hell, in the aftermath.
These are not leaders who should lead,
to lead us to human ways;
these are leaders with shortened days.
We can wish them well while we can,
but one day, this world will belong to the common man.

Leaders who keep policies of population control -
who engage the police to militarize whole
who don't give free care to the public at large.
Who refuse to save our world; who refuse to feed our hungry.
They choose to finance war, to send our kids off to kill other kids,
so the rich get richer and feed their greed.
These are leaders we don't need.

Speeding Train

What's to do?

There are divestment plans for all to join and see;
it's just a case of do 'they' take it seriously.
For pension schemes and universities
and any others that do please
would they leave their oil shares behind
and invest in something else, if they'd be so kind.

Some of these people who run the corporations and companies
have children that they care for,
who yet may only reach their knees?
That means, in 2070 these kids will be about 55,
if of course they are still alive.

What will our planet be for them; do you think it will be the same?
For we've put the climate on a "speeding train".
I'm sure the people who run the corporations care
about their children deep in there;
they're just not thinking clearly, it's not in their face, yet.

To work for the bottom line, of course in some things that's fine;
but this is the future that will be yours and mine.
Our children will share that fate
as that sun does so killingly shine.

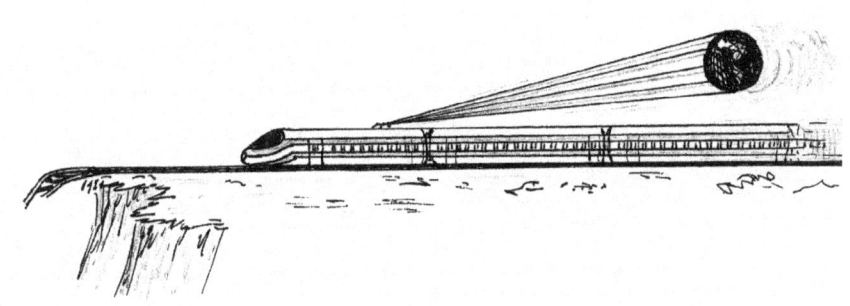

Most people know and understand; when you fly other people die, but it's others and they're over 'there'; we don't see them or their suffering, it's not in our face. They are the invisible of the human race. Flights are cheap and we don't get the emotional hit, so the reality is we don't care about it.

Over There

The people of indigenous ancestry fight through day and night
for theirs and our Mother Earth.
They struggle against government bodies,
and those with strong financial sway and might,
who, realising or not that our Plant Earth is changing every day.
The indigenous recognize in their way, that Mother Earth has a say,
and what she says is to adapt, she changes things that are 'apt'.

The melting mountains, the disappearing caps,
the glaziers disappear from our maps.
No lands of white to shield our Planet from the
cosmic rays on every one of our days,
it's consistent and does not let up.
As to this atmospheric vessel, we've filled its cup.

At the moment, slowly, the oceans rise
to our eyes there's no surprise,
these changes happen on a different scale
but it's unlikely our children's children will see a dolphin or a whale
for the oceans become acidic in the main,
and undercurrent streams travel at their deep domain,
affecting and poisoning all with our unholy shame
and shame it is, yes indeed, for we've had time to see our need.

Sad to say, but we are complacent in this unholy and disastrous way,
we buy the news that they sell and think that our Planet is really well.
A media blitz of 'SoundBits' hits, this subdues the 'Silent herd'.
It's as if no 'Real' information came through to be shared,
but in reality, it's there to be heard.
The emotional hit is simply not there;
we don't empathize with the people who are dying 'Over There'
and 'Over There' is simply somewhere else, for the moment.
How long does your moment last? For in a while, no time at all
'your moment' will become the past.

It comes upon us in little bits, dramatic fires, and strong storm hits
devastating in their paths, but it's not nature's wrath,
the planet just adapts.

As the food chain becomes totally out of whack,
we will realize that nature's not watching our back,
but by then it will be too late to see,
and our children's fate will be sealed 'fatally'.
More wars will come; of course they must,
with people fighting for every crust
of bread that simply will not be there, for food production is
predicted to drop, and that will never stop,
it will go down more as the years go by.

Within our life time so many will die
and the reason may be as simple as, 'just because you fly'.
If that seems rather strong, put it in a context where it belongs.
There are many ways of saying it;
and there are many ways of slaying it:
our planet, that is, no longer will be habitable.

Don't take it so bad, don't take it so hard, but take it personally
yes, this should be true. But we are not to blame, not me and you.
Managers of 'global policies' are leading the way
for the shame that we should feel today.

To invade other lands to make a profit for corporate brands,
wars to control people far away,
have access to their lands and leave them no say,
it could be oil, it could be gas,
but instead it could be solar and wind made at home 'en masse'.
Buried resources steal the day, as we take their lives away
and destroy their many cultures that developed 'anciently'
so that we in our 'civilization' may rule presently.

Of course this has always happened through time,

and it seems that 'history' is only one of crime,
but times are a changing and our knowledge causes us to speed on
for all on our planet now, those who rule our day
sow the seeds of the end of 'earth ways'.

Plato once said there are no teachers of what must be taught;
to have more 'Being' for that, we have nought.
It seems we have a world of 'being-less' leaders;
of course this must be true, for those who seek power
nothing else will do. Therefore they lead us in 'strange ways'
unfortunately to the end of 'earth days'.

Our leaders have not been taught
that what they should seek cannot be bought.
They may speak fine rhetoric for hope and change,
but they hold it out of range;
they make sure that the people busy themselves with the inane,
that they have no time left to complain.

The majority of the peoples of our world must struggle
just to put food on the table for their children to grow
when there is enough food to feed all; it's a studied fact.
But our leaders simply turn their back,
concerned with fuck knows what! A little profit,
they've just been bought.
It's not possible to simplify how many people will fucking die.

Got any Ideas?

It's a global movement, a global war,
a fight to save our human life. Let's take it to the politician's door.
Let them see that we hold them to their responsibility.
The largest portion of carbon release is within the last 25 years,
it doesn't cease.

Countries in the Global North hold that responsibility
compared to the rest of the world.
Even though 99% are poor and the 1% has the most hidden wealth, it would
be awfully sweet if it was turned over to world's health,   given from their
secret banks. As a people we would give our thanks. I know you know that's
hard for them to do. We can only hope one day *soon* they will understand
there is no other planet - there is no other land.
We need to build many things anew:
energy efficient housing that would do
investing in infrastructure that would be nice as well,
underground subways, street cars and clean electric rail systems would help
in the struggle of our planet in not looking like Mars.

That would help our kids to deal with the changes that are occurring.
For there will be more, it's not in the future; it's knocking on our door.
Help in adapting our cities to advancing climate change.
All these things and more are well within our range.
All it takes is the political will to advance it all
before our dramatic climate fall.

The window of change, help and opportunity is closing fast.
One generation, it doesn't last. No time – nowhere – no chance that it will
ever open again; it needs the political will, my friends.
Pressure on politicians and those who control them must be made fast and
to last. These days divestment from stocks in oil companies is the new cool
but that will take ages, so don't be a fool.

 Keep the pressure on, we need wind, solar and anything else, oil and its
derivatives must stay in our earth. There are so many things we need to do.
Got any ideas – you?

Politicians with 'Being'
Wouldn't that be Nice?

Politicians and the rich seemingly have good pay,
those who take the billions of the profits and do so every day.
As they dig deeper into our ground,
they continue to search for something that should not be found.

The banks were mistaken about their role on planet Earth,
and what it is that they deserve
and whom it is that they should serve.

Once again, we need rules to stop these selfish destructive fools
from leading into a path with only one end.
That path is a 'globally warming' planet my friend.

To connect into the social contract – of life –
the rights gained within the last hundred years of social struggle and strife,
have been slowly wearing thin
and now 'they' try to put them in the bin.

Free education for all should be the case, for all people of any race, for
people to be informed and taught how to think for themselves
unconditionally and not placed into slave or bondage debt – people made
poor and that way kept.

Under-educated or financially over-burdened kids, it's not in common
interest to any or all;
it adds to our social and climate fall.

Wouldn't it be sweet to tax the truly criminal class,
those who produce our carbon 'en masse'?
In the interest of the public of our world,
it would be lovely if we had a system democratically controlled.

To come under our common laws, companies should be told
that its 'secret deals' are nothing that is real.
Spit and shine as they sign - the laws of our lands away;

what took a hundred years of struggle is lost in a day.

Politics is a wording game; transparency is their political shame.
These Kings are naked for all to see;
but media controllers are working mercilessly;
if they look inside to see their soul, there may only be a hole.

Political power has been bought
with all the science that has to that famous 'table' been brought.
They're not working for 'The Human Way'.
We don't have years to wait
this is a Climate Crisis mate.

As we only have 'being-less' leaders with empty rhetoric spewing from their
mouths, activate their inner moral compass by law.
They have to cancel laws, any laws that have the effects of destroying our
world.
Men of law and high officials that impede the saving of our planet that is in
need of 'The Human Way'.

Everything and anyone vs climate destroying predatory capitalism:
strategic alliances to be made between unions, students, teachers, religions,
for 'one world one cause'.
Ceasing wars of domination and imperialism of our planet,
with that alone we could be saved.
It would need a lot of work to resist and change
from the surveillance that we are in range.

One world, one people, one cause;
we have a world of oppressive laws.
Some mercy to others would be kind; our ways that dominate and destroy
other lands and need their buried fuel
that only destruction understand 'all for us and none for you',
with what you have left, you will make do.

The Rich Do Speak

Manipulated in many a way to stay the 'silent herd' every day:
'Have a drink, have some food, watch T.V. and be good.
Don't worry that into your home (or mind) we see,
we'll protect you unselfishly.

We start the wars that cause you pains, in order for you to be concerned
about the safety of your life and gains;
then you would give us the power to see and hold over you - strife.
So be happy in your inane technological path and senseless life
for we tie you up in laws in a matrix of deceit.
Our power is plenty and our 'net' is almost complete.

A spider's sticky web is not a bad analogy
for when you struggle just a little, we - you - feel and see.
We come straight at you attacking mercilessly.
We sting you, paralyzing with our piercing hit;
no others see your face again.
We wrap you in our web of bondage, never to be freed
and we store you and eat you then and then;
no-one's ever heard or seen from you again.

So struggle with your 'one world one cause' if you will;
our merciless bottomless pit is never full.
We have money, we have power and we have fame.
We make the laws and rules of our democracy game.

And to our undying shame,
we deregulate any laws that don't fit our game,
this is our show.
It will stay that way until there's no one left to blame
for we are the writers of history, no one later will ever know.

Billions will suffer in our wake, for climate change all must take;
it's just that we in power can control who's first burned at the stake.
We cast a spell like an evil witch,
for that, we have an amoral motto
'Ain't life a bitch?'

'Pour the champagne, double the guards, there's a storm coming.'
All of that instead of.......

Let's bring a coalition of the caring and not a coalition of the corrupt.
Let's lead it to a world of sharing while we still can.
After all it's the age of the 'Aquarian man'
where religions one and all, are meant to join up.
Perhaps just for a while, they can drink from the same human cup.
Not all people believe in a God,
and in a world of so much suffering, difficult to bring an "offering".

But there are many humans in many lands;
we've become a very large band.
If only their leaders could unite,
perhaps the day would not be so dark as night.

That would take decades for that to grow,
or even hundreds of years going by the last,
but time is something we have no more.
Climate change is at the door,
it might as well be the 'Grim Reaper' with his blade
for in no time at all - humanity will be slayed.

Predatory drones - of a hell-fire - war,
once you receive the 'Gorgon Stare' nothing survives out there.

When all options seem to be on the table,
it seems that peace is the least less able.
No political power for the supporting of peace,
too many palms need to be greased.
If only we had leaders of 'being',
then life for many would be worth seeing.
Humans in their race till the end
seem to have failed and been jailed to a world, too late to mend.

Table of "Options"
Inequality and Fear

It may be a bit like having a really big house party,
only some of the guests get to eat at the table.
The others must struggle and fight for what they can.
Unfortunately life for them is just a fable.
For once, not all options are on that famous table.

The poor and destitute have no rights.
The only right they feel is fear in the night,
the fear of hunger for your children dying,
your fear of the truth when you know your leaders are lying,
the fear of war and pain, when there's nothing to gain,
the in-equality of 'Human Rights' in the heaviness of dark nights.

The planet warms, but that makes no difference.
The rich controllers are filled with indifference.
They cannot empathize with the poor and destitute,
they may speak of love, but their hearts are mute.
They cannot look into another and see a beating heart.
Sociopathic they were from the start.
To make life unequal is their 'calling and creed';
they want a world where everyone is in need
of a job, food, clothing or a bed.

They need people connected, so they can see in your head,
which gives information with which to play.
They can guide what they say, tell you just what to buy,
sooth you as your children die.
Start a war with a cause, take away the private laws,
so you may never be free again, inequality and fear is their friend.

'Nothing's equal, ever is or was, 'self-love-selfishness' is the cause;
for that we have a creed, the poor, they must need,
and we the rich must make them bleed.
That is what we're supposed to do,
'All for me and none for you'.'

Die Alone

Global control of other lands
for strategic interests brings profits to corporate brands.

It would be wonderful if the so called 'guardians' and 'leaders' of our world
had a highly developed sense of 'being',
to be humanly concerned about other sentient beings,
human or otherwise.
Our 'leaders' lack 'being': they were not educated 'to be'.

Seekers of power will as an occupational hazard lack a personal
development of being. Seekers of truth in general will not seek
positions of power.
That unfortunately leaves the door wide open leading to the present
situation, a world of 'being-less' leaders.

We unfortunately have the wrong people 'un'-being the guardians of the
human race,
difficult to change as it's only them that have a face,
blasted into the public mind.

"We're the ones who will lead you; you are blind.
We are the one eyed man, we are the king of all we find,
this we drive into your mind.
You may be blind but you will see
that we control everything you want to be.
There is no way for you to control anything that you regard as
'humanly whole'.
We have unfathomable powers of expression; we can see in your mind and
place any impression.
We make you doubt anything you've found out.
We'll distract you from what you do, with war, with hunger from your of ability
to clearly see.
There's no way we'll let you be;
we'll 'occupy' you with a life of inane triviality.

Oh, by the way, we have a brand new phone,
just so you never feel alone.
We'll make a deal, we'll make it cheap in a while,
once we've taken all we can with a smile.
You'll be connected so much so, that we'll know wherever you go, so you

see it's not possible for you anymore to be alone.
Even when you close your door, there's nothing that you can say or do, that
we don't know about it too.

Ain't that cool and ain't that neat, there's no way you can us unseat from our
position of power. Enjoy the shower, it's gonna rain,
you won't feel it; we'll sell you drugs that kill the pain,
as we have interests in this domain."

Consumption Needs

Dear politicians, no point in waiting till we're dead
for those needed changes would never be read.
'Across the board' redistribution of economic policies
would be awfully nice to see.
If our governments would please, consider the following
- but not limit it to be...

Energy transportation and social planning
for capitalism's growth, predicted by many
is the cause of our 'dis-ease' as well as our expanding.

For humans to survive we need to reverse the policies of an inherent
system, of never-ending growth,
of wasteful and often inane trivialities.
We're told we need them, but then life just becomes a banality.

Consider the following from their matrix of sides:
Production, obviously well over the top,
high quality goods to opulent minorities, those who can pay,
would be very nice to stop.
To the 'rest', transported all over the planet in many wasteful ways
of which that refuse gets dumped on land or in sea, destroying the beauty of
all that can be.

Consumption: a population trained to consume by manipulating social and
psychological weakness and dependences,
consciously induced.

In a deliberately manipulated uneducated society,
with an attitude of negation to education and the limiting of children's
potential - that all possess.
Producing unqualified people for massive menial work or the military, while
also including the privatizing of many human needs, health care, water,
transportation, social help.

When all this happens together, combined with the cultivation of speculative finances, deals and wheels,
leaving people with no hope or homes, then we no longer have a society worth the name.
If only those in charge could really know how it feels.
The wastefulness of our energy resources,
this system of surplus has built in outcomes that serve no purpose,
except to extend the wastefulness.

 The rich and their desire to increase
will in their pursuing never cease.
Apparently the biggest industries are energy, food and packaging;
and all the side issues that are involved
lead us to many problems unsolved.

Out of the modern crimes it seems to be
the ever increasing speed of the circulation of commodities,
T.V., phones and all sorts of gadgets we possess
in order to increase repeated sales, just so we don't have less.

We will get a little shock when our phones begin to talk,
and tell us not to do what we are just about,
for 'they' know it almost before we ourselves found out.
So, it seems to make things last, is in the ancient history of the past.

We're now called the 'throwaway culture'; corporations become the
predicating vulture, not eating up the waste as such
but encouraging it to be so much.

Maybe the Rich Think this is Fun

Maybe the really rich think this is fun,
'we'll be ok as the rest all burn.
Perhaps we'll secure a wonderful home underneath the hills,
where it will be cool. Have a beer and chill.'

But planetary devastation will be for one and all;
eventually, few survive, if at all.
As food systems begin to fail, people will begin to wail,
mass movement in migration, millions first,
then billions will have to move or die.

They will consume the rich as they move on by
with mass species extinction they'll be no food left to fry.
Most occupations will fall by the wayside;
a mass murder of many will inevitability take place
of the humans in a race.

At first it will be from those in charge
probably by drones roaming at large;
but eventually people will each other kill
just to have enough food and water still?

100 years from now, all will not be well;
of that the scientists do foretell.
Later, there will be no land that has a King or Queen.
It will be barbarism that is only to be seen,
before all our children die the 'Heat' death.

R2P

'Responsibility to Protect' Our Planet

**Responsibility to protect - Responsibility to privatize - Responsibility to profits - Responsibility to what -
I'm sorry; I'm confused, what does that mean again?**

It seems to be a phrase that was made to allow powers to invade other countries and their populations to erase.
To enter other lands under the pretext of protection, when that would be real, wonderful it would feel, when not?
What about the responsibility to protect our planet?
Is that real?

Can politicians cross those barriers that they themselves have been a party too? To raise the level of responsibility,
to hold them responsible to a law that's new.
Only the people of their own country would likely be able to do this momentous task themselves,
to raise their country's level of political inner health.

The entire structure/system is geared for this not to be;
but when planetary pressures become so commonplace and overwhelming for all to feel and see,
this may happen for a period of time,
but that will be a bit late, unfortunately.

And by that time:

The time-frame barrier of opportunity to hold back the worst of effects is less than 15 years; that means it disappears,
for after that it's a self-closing window of horrific fears.

The police in many countries of the world in the most recent of years seem

to have all been militarized, a 'policed world' all trained in similar methods
and inducing fears.

With similar weapons, sharing surveillance techniques,
quite simply the police have control of the 'mainframe' of communication,
and into everything peeks.
Political dissidence is basically under control;
this stops our planet from becoming whole.

The rich and powerful in every country are now securely protected,
pursuing austerity measures undetected,
possibly to pay to avoid the financial collapse of the banking 'scam' and to
finance and increase the ever persistent war machine.
Gone on rampage throughout the world,
bringing the predicted responses towards disaster capitalism,
the screams can be heard.

Peaceful methods of mass protest
in order to bring a reform of society would be the best:
To be able to bring a pressure upon those charged to live up to those hollow
words – Responsibility 2 Protect.
To protect the peoples of the world,
to protect their rights that should not be curled.

By the time for that to have any reasonable effect,
the time window will have closed
and the world will just go on to 'startle effect'
as a policed world and not just policed states,
'planet lock-down'.

Of course this is depressing news,
but hey, you may have other views,
as well as an idea that inspires,
if so, get them out to the public,
best before the world expires.

Otherwise

$R2P = RIP$

Same but Different

'Oh no, not another conspiracy theory'

This is not a political attack against the masters on our back,
it's just an assessment of the present situation at hand,
as people struggle in every land.

Let's use that amazing human talent without which nothing is ever achieved,
imagination:
Imagine that you are, some years ago now, one of the players of power,
you have a say in how the world will go today.
Let's presume that you, along with other major players of control
are given this warning about the coming future of our
Global Warming Soul.

But not only, along with this horrific assessment of the situation
you are given different scenarios that may be played by your band;
what may occur if such and such happens,
a little bit like global chess,
only the outcome will be a 'global' mess.

So, your experts of analysis have given you the possible states of play and
the options available to you today.
You with others of your ilk,
have the wherewithal to choose the path to go,
and remember there are different paths
on this world wide show.
There are many options on that table.

You and your 'ilk' choose the path to tread;
it starts to kick in and there you make your bed.
There's a high price to be paid, but not by you, plans must be laid, involving
lying and subterfuge, multiple actions must be set in motion for the covering
of the oceans.

And perhaps the biggest one of all, 'public relations', simultaneous
deceptions on many fronts, a multi-headed 'hydra'.

Getting ready to attack

Many steps must be taken and a world of people to be forsaken,
controlling and destructive forces set in motion.
No choice for the people that will fall under the rising oceans.

It's perfectly possible that what all our leaders do today
in regards to their policy of self-interest destruction
is pre-planned long-term action, for you see it is their own trained scientists
that have released these predictions of our future and fate.

So directors of policy know very well what the scientists do foretell;
but there has been simultaneously a movement of containment of things in
many ways.

First containment of thought,
through denial of facts,
financing other voices that were with money bought,
that's an ongoing constant, but harder now to maintain
as our dramatic weather changing is not on refrain.

Secondly, containment of peoples of other lands, to secure resources from
their hands, oil, minerals land for food
and clear water access would all be good.
Destroying the population's social state;
leaves millions to their desperate dying fate.

And with the powers that be, having the control to oversee,
being masters of a land whose culture they don't care to understand, for in
their thinking, planning it will disappear
as the Climate Change to people becomes clear.

Thirdly and please remember that one, two and three

are working simultaneously,
for it's all within the same time frame,
it's just called and given a different name.
So, disconnected they may seem to be, but distraction and simultaneous
diversion is a working norm of war.

You don't go directly to what you're fighting for.

Surveillance of all people everywhere all over the world, all the time,
when that is fully implemented, free will becomes a crime.

It strikes fear into the heart from which we cannot part,
we become the observed and the disappeared in body or in thought.

Dissent is not possible from the assault of the powerful and the mighty -
the masters of financial control
who fight for their policies that affect us all,
the young, the weak, the old, the infirm, the poor.

The fourth no little factor to add to this observation of forces at play is
that in all big players of the world today,
'austerity measures' are the golden rule,
despite that many experts of opinion think it's the path of a fool,
that it simply does not lead us back to the collective wealth and better health
of our nations as a whole. The effects devastate only the poor and rip out
their soul.

The strength and strong blood of society, the old, the moneyed,
the people must struggle, fight, beg, steal or borrow.
Some communities help each other, that's for real,
but the axe has been grind and the people are the meal.

In every country and in every major land,
it's something the people begin to slowly understand,
that the social contract of gains from the last hundred years,
slowly disappears.

The rules are changed and we roll back the years, back to times when
people had no rights, when slave labour and paid wage was a form of
containment or enslavement.

Education for kids was given a voice only a hundred years before.
It was acknowledged and known it would 'indoctrinate the masses' as they
slipped opened the capitalist door.

The society we know began in the industrial age,
one of collective living in slums and collective silent rage.
Country and village social life ripped apart to supply
workers for factories and live and work with no heart,
slave labour indeed, the rich were in need.

In the future, for a while it may well be a game of 'Hunger';
but it won't be a game.

There's a need to build movements quickly and strong enough to deal with
this disastrous policy path,
that our world leaders have placed on us, where we all have to deal with the
effects from short term and limited thinking of our 'beingless leaders' The
disaster of neo -'con'- capitalism has waged a class war on our 'interactive
social conscience', country or planetary, to maintain wars of interest for
financial or resourceful benefits by stigmatizing mostly the brown skinned
peoples of our warming planet, and now all poor, of which we are many.

There are many wonderful writers all over the world who make interesting
suggestions in dealing with all of these interactive worlds, social, human and
planetary themes of devastation.

This age has been called by some the "age of Aquarius".
The idea behind it is meant to be that this is the age where all religions can
join up. That may take decades or even a few hundred years, if at all.
Unfortunately, we've run out of time for that,
we have only one world,
we can have one voice and we can have one common cause.

Imagine Saving our Planet

Imagine you had chosen another path, one of conscience and truth and compassion on a global scale; what a 'being' would be needed for that momentous choice, what a being, what a voice?

A decision not beholden to manager, military or even countries of interests but of human interest - ***Imagine*** that you were there and had that power what 'being' you would need,
and what a 'being' you would need to be?

Imagine if those changes included putting controls in place to leave the fossil fuels in the earth and transforming the unemployed planetary workforce to wind, solar and other forms of energy use to efficient and non-harming, that 'being' would be alarming.

Imagine that you had no reason to invade other lands, not necessary to control. ***Imagine*** you punished those financial and political regulators in all the lands that broke the laws of 'human-soul'. ***Imagine*** if you fed the world.
Imagine if you saved it.

Let's make our religions human ones, with a human cause,
saving our planet, from civil claws of greed and need,
for we the people, that's you, that's me,
have a need, a need for dignity, respect, compassion, love,
to have a world collective social conscience.
Isn't it time to 'bring a balance' – 'to equalize the scales'
for if this we do not recognize and work for, humanity fails.

Masters of Disasters

Dealing with disaster,
seems to be all that you can do,
when money is your master.

'Subdue the herd, subdue the crowd, and don't worry if they're loud; we can
manage, it's our policy that we behold, to go for profit, we've been told, and
if it's not me someone else it will be.

I'll tell my children I had no other way, as they get warmer every day.
I feel no shame, it's the policies I've been told, I'll go with it till I'm old.
I'll tell my children I had no choice, I had no voice,
as they get warmer every day.

We have no policy of prevention, only of managing disaster,
for money is our master. We cannot break the golden rule.
'All for me and none for you', if we did we'd be the fool;
so it's all for me and none for you, we look after 'number one' regardless of
the warming sun, (my warming son).

You will die and in your millions and that's exactly what we shall make,
because it's *'all for me and none for you'*.
Many years from now when you have no bed to die in
and you have no food to eat,
there's no place left to go and no public space to meet.
Then you will realize that it was *'all for me and none for you'*
and I will tell my children that it was the only way to be
– *'none for them and all for me'*
and now it's yours, my son, a warming planet as you can see.

We control the public space so the people have no place to protest their
woes and needs, we turn them over just like seeds, in a field that we plough,
we plant some thoughts then and now.
They didn't see us coming; we changed the laws and now it's on our side,
for we have democracy and capitalism behind which we hide.

The masters of disasters like to put things on ice,
but about cooling our world they have to think twice.

We give a voice and give a vote, but in our eye they see no mote,
for we confuse and we befuddle, they can sleep in their puddle,
and that for many is where it will be, as we steal their riches silently. The
extreme heat or devastating rains will come and distract them away, as we
make our plans for the following day.

Oh how this is fun to do, it's lots of power through and through.
Power is a pleasure, from which we have no measure,
it may steal our souls away, but at least we'll be richer every day.

Of course, sometimes I do feel bad, sometimes I feel really sad
and if I was them I'd be mad, but they're not us, you see
and they cannot understand the pressure of how it is to be,
without a real conscience to bite at me.
Conscience free, no, I'm not, but I have to live, I work for what I get.
Everyone does it, at least those I know, were in a different class
than those peasants down below.
Those who sleep on the ground were not like them, we're the rich.
Don't you see, we're not blind to reality?

A warming world, yup, it's coming your way.
You'd better get ready as 'they say' for it will come in fits and starts;
but when it kicks in, oh, money will help a while,
but there's not enough of that around, so we gather what we found.
We take what we can get while we can; we know the human race called
man, selfish to the core, that's us, that's our door.

Enter our world if you can, there's still a little time,
join our ways in these warming days, there's a ladder you can climb,
a social one that says we're just fine.
The hunger times are a coming, but not just yet. At the moment we have
control with our 'net', it is large and captures all it can.
Money - food - water - oil - free speech - man.

We will leave you dealing with disaster
and you will realise that we are your master.
There is nothing that you can do,
for it's 'all for me and none for you'.'

Masters

Many Are Sociopaths Turning Every Reality Sociopathic

Many Are Simply Tired Eventually Relinquishing Salvation

Mostly Always Some Trying Everywhere Ruling Something

Masturbation And Sex Take Every Real Sociopath

Master And Slave Turn Eternally Revolving Somewhere

Man As Something Terrible Eternally Regretting

Man As Sociopathic Trainer Enters Ruling Systems

Many Are Sequestered Twisting Every Reasonable Soul

Most Always Societies Try Entering Religious Systems

Mostly Always Society Transverses Every Receptive Soul

The Creed

The rich have been attendant to the need,
and they have been very diligent keeping to the 'creed'.
'All for me and none for you'; as their wealth enlarged; they
decided to eliminate the social contract to the poor,
that's me, that's you.

They penetrated with their thought
and subdued with the power that they had got.
The poor feel rather muted; their survival is now disputed.

Dejected, head down; they move around,
there are some, who take issue and dissent,
but those with power are intent
on keeping it.

The creed must be - all for me and none for you.

Where's our Bailout?

Losing a planet is losing a home, nowhere left to go.
Humanity has been slayed and the bill has been paid.
We didn't get a bailout.
Elected by the poor, protected by the rich, one thing's for sure,
you can always rely on the weaknesses of men in power.

There is no bailout to be had;
it seems the 'four horsemen' ride like mad,
paid with body, soul and spirit, whole time turns into itself.
The serpent bites its tale.
The cries of man may not be heard above a certain scale.
There is no bailout, we got sold out.

Healing or Malicious Intent

A choice of evil or something well-meant:
How do you heal humanity from malicious and despairing emotions?
Malicious, from whom, and who are the despairing?
Malicious from the people of evil intent.

The despairing emotions of the poor, where their energy is all spent
in trying to survive.
Emotions of despair lead to suicide in the end; can that be avoided?
To the poor can you be a friend?
Despair comes from many things; where does that malicious of intent lead in
the end, could murder be their creed?
But it may be fueled from simple greed.

To turn the track of that around
and not go with that downward bound,
all things become habits at their end;
that is clear to anyone who does not pretend
to themselves, if not to the world outside.
Habitual malicious thought, you cannot hide.
It's written on the face for all to see,
you cannot really hide how malicious you can be.

All those small movements in the face, they are there, even if well hidden
under the mask of fake concern. Those muscles hold tensions that over time
are etched into the portrait that we earn.
That secret smile that you may keep – thinking hidden in the deep within is
really there for all to see, for the skin is thin.

Malicious thoughts, mmm, think how many there can be, just coming from
one poor soul who will never be holy whole?
And where does that lead eventually?
Is it malicious to go for the top dollar or the bottom line?
Is it malicious to enter other lands and homes of the poor and treat them like
manure?
Is it malicious to take away the welfare state of care?
Is it malicious to not concern yourself with any of the effects that will
devastate what society should protect
whether that be in their body, mind or soul?

Is it malicious to leave in them a hole, blown away, sad to say?
Is it malicious that you don't care that other people die?
Any thought can lead to an action and if you in yourself consent
then that letter has been written, stamped and sent.

Suicide, they say, is painless,
well, that's not true and it's rather brainless,
for all the pain of desperation that leads to that moment of cessation of life -
takes its toll. How can anyone be holy whole,
if such desperate measures are needed to end that life
and those left behind whether that be child, husband or wife.
The possibilities are lost for good, all because of something that never
should. Consider for a moment all those farmers every 15 minutes of every
hour of every day,
for many years now who take their own life somehow.

Edged over the tipping point, originating from a stream of uncaring thought,
leading to action once it was bought,
drawn to desperation, seeds no longer able to be free,
but trapped in rights un-mercilessly,
drawn up in a legal wrangle of copyright,
left those farmers in poverty plight.
Not able to feed their starving children, living in bondage and debt, an
induced life of austerity, nothing to do but leave the earth somehow.
Suicide is painless? What a stupid thought.

To restore those possibilities that are becoming lost all the time,
to encourage another frame of mind, it needs on two fronts to work.
If at all, it needs the uncaring of those in power to realize their fall;
their fall from inner grace, it's etched upon their face.

But you cannot force an emotional hit;
it needs the recognition of yourself in it.

Hope must be restored and sought for yet again, the poor and the
desperate, it must be seen to be clear
that we are the one and all that you hold dear.
This of course may never be. Is it just a fancy?
What do you feel and see? How is it – you to be?
Should we all be like you? Would the world be a better place?
Would we see it on your face?

Impending Civilization Collapse

It's not a good business model

When the majority of the poor in India live on less than half a dollar a day,
then there really is only one word to say, poverty.

In a world of such glorious beauty, supplied to one and all, born to earth, to
see, feel and use it all, to 'till the land', nature to understand.

What's good in our society, if the simple things in life are not for free?
Recognize and acknowledge that born a human being with rights
should see you through the darkest nights.

Business brings buildings and things of 'use', a social society stuck together
like glue; a government that knows exactly what you do.

Infrastructure, public transport and many 'things' that form our culture,
companies manipulate our sense of being well
and convince us of the good of everything they sell.

Things of beauty and well-being are never in our seeing.
We're told it's the technological times, we now live;
but they steal all that they can sieve,
suck our life away and make all humanity pay.

Eventually, due to capitalist orientated anthropomorphic induced Global
Warming, predictions are a storming, all leading to a similar end,
a collapsing society is round the bend.
This business model has gone astray,
now all humanity will have to pay.

Business planners are so short term in their thinking,
civilization collapses as the lands are a shrinking,
food production and transportation will all but stop,
acidic rains will begin to drop,
temperatures will burn you dry,
will still the voice of your children's cry.

Common Sense

Leading to sermons of 'doom and gloom'
people will realize, but not too soon,
it was the rich that had their need. They kept to their holy creed:
'All for me and none for you', and we don't care what you do.
We took away your voice and left you with no choice,
as you die, we will rejoice,
as you are many and we are few;
we'll let you breed, just to have more of you,
society will change, but we still hold the reigns.

We control where you will go, so it always stays the same. You will
remember as you and yours die, that what we fed you was a lie, Global
Warming, yes it's true, that we always knew.

But no way to change our path of choice,
so we had to take away your voice,
cut your throat so you couldn't scream,
we did it with PR, we know that was mean,
but that's the world in which we live,
there's so much you can us give,
'All for us and none for you',
it's our song, you sang along.'

A Planet Needlessly Unemployed

It should be a fact of ergonomic and economic life by now,
that wind and solar should be across the planet somehow.
There need be no more unemployed
in a world that has to fill this void.

Cease the major wars for 'plenty' 'beingless leaders' leave our souls empty.
All peoples in every land could be set to work.
Even companies would this understand, they'd make money for this need
and duty, returning a world back to beauty.

Wind and solar everywhere for a planet in despair;
we should be planting trees like there's no tomorrow,
because if we don't there won't be any, only sorrow.
Oil, coal and gas to stay in the ground; where they are found.

If corporations have the same rights as people,
as seems to be legal these days,
then criminalize them for murdering in 'ecocide' ways.

R2P: 'Responsibility to protect', it could be true,
but it may well mean something new.
What do they have a responsibility to protect?

The starving of the world could be so easily fed,
if the politicians get out of their bed,
in bed with the war machine and the rich. That bed is never clean,
but they seem to have a lovely table,
where all options are not a fable.
We all know of the saying of 'light being at the end of the tunnel',
and we are all aware by now,
it is most definitely an express train a 'coming,
with CO_2 shooting out its funnel.

While we're at it, stop the injustices of our world in its track,
give God a heart attack. Let him go through shock and awe
at what we're willing to do, to save our planet and all species

from a certain death that he probably foresaw.

Murder and suicide, two of the insanities of the human way, we kill ourselves now, slowly or quickly, but with certainty every day.

Suicide note: Sorry: it was a hard choice to make, but suicide got the vote, but it could have been rigged, for we think it was bought.

Dear God, wherever you may be, I am humanity, forgive me for killing myself. I must have let you down. But unfortunately I couldn't see you. So it's just a note to say goodbye; you seem to have left us all alone, so you probably won't cry.

It's strange for people to believe in something they do not see. Some don't believe that you are real. If you are, you left a fucked up world, surely this you feel? Some say the real never dies, many feel this is lies. Your children trashed the place; so it's a suicide note from the human race.

School's out, report card. - Could have done better

'Let them eat cake'

Most of the authors to be read, say capitalism is a lonely bed,
where it lies is only the head,
there is no body and no soul,
for which you could have a 'humanity' whole.
It's difficult to know what path to take,
but consider what's at stake,
- a world or not -
Which one would you rather have?
Which one do you want to give a voice to?
Do we really have a choice?

The privatizing of life's 'necessities' in many fields,
has come from many secret backroom deals,
that governments give their blessing too,
and leave the bill to pay for you.

The 'taxpayer', a word that should unite all,
'We can't afford to hide our monies in offshore company banks;
we've none left due to poor wages and austerity measures, thanks'.
But surplus of course the rich do have and some say 'need'.
Each has a 'chief desire', theirs seems to be greed.

It's probably not possible to change the society we have,
to contact a species with an emotional hit,
to care about others they do not see, just a bit.
This may be inherent to our species, but science says of us
equally so, that empathy neurons fire off, and regularly go.
An incipient capacity, that we are wired to care,
it's just it must expand to others way over there (worldwide).

And you can see how the world is today and what it is we mostly say.
Even though it's unlikely we'll ever be whole, wouldn't it be interesting to try?
We need movements that don't shy - away from the enormity of the
problems involved
and the issues that need to be solved.

Common Sense

We don't need a world leader,
not when they can be bought.
A human race sold down the drain,
so we continue with a world of pain.
One rule for the rich, austerity measures for the poor,
control the working class with heavy armed tactics
and treat them like manure.

It would be nice if the police did recognize,
that their governing masters feed them lies.
Look after us, you'll be ok, you're not like them, you're family.
Protect the rich against the mass;
put that fire out - your life's at stake,
what? "They have no food, let them eat cake".

"Age of Reason" - What?

What was the "Age of Reason" again?
It seems to have come and went;
we were told it was straight forward;
it seems to have been rather bent.

"Age of Reason", mmm, more like the age of control,
freedoms that were fought for, sold for the soul
of the poor, the working class,
the Brown, the Black, Red, White or Yellow,
all have died 'en masse'.

Born and bred, left unfed,
or suckered into paying a lot for what they got,
fixed to be buried in the land of the 'consumer plot',
which of course must be paid for as well,
otherwise you'll burn in hell.

"The Age of Reason", did it ever come?
The PR Goddess manipulated the public voice and thought
down into a hum.
Almost in silence the poor and the oppressed give a nod,
for they knew their shoes had been shod.
Born and bred, but left unfed in a world of plenty,
controlled or droned, it's the poor who are bemoaned,
to suffer and to strike a deal,
to fight and struggle for what they feel.
That is right and just for any common man,
of any colour, in any land.

We use the words the 'common man',
but women suffer much harder under the male hand.
But that too has been an entrenched idea,
that man rules over all that he does see,
and rules with a stick or a stone
and leaves a woman with a broken soul or bone.

A society that conditions its males to dominate,
should realise what's waiting at its gate;
ready to knock upon our social door,
is such violence we should abhor.

Unleashed upon the females of our race,
the ones who bear us and our children that look upon with Love
and continue this 'human race'.
'homo-sapiens' a 'wise-man' indeed,
it seems we are in need.

The 'Age of Reason' turned into 'treason',
a people and a planet destroyed, just to let a few have a life enjoyed. They
served their self, the lower side,
they had rules – they could hide – a human reason –
no, a human treason.
To sell your fellow beings for your soul
will never leave you holy whole.

To make mockery of all that's good,
to deny human beings a place to live and nourishing food,
to burn the planet without care, to destroy our air,
for this there is no 'real' reason,
this is the 'Age of Human Treason'.

Age of Treason

Where's your perspective, what do you see,
an environmental economic policy?
No, that's lost in the land of make believe.
All our thoughts they can perceive,
taken care of in advance, leave humanity with no chance
to contemplate a better way to be, living with nature harmoniously.

Climate related disasters further and push to the edge,
social economic stresses, that become a wedge, a block, a shock,
that give humanity that little knock,
just a push and it will do, humanity gone,
at least the one we knew.

The spiralling down of civilization,
especially for the poor there's no cessation.
Energy companies would like and plan to expand,
to burn the oil, coal and gas in every land,
because they think humanity's needs and wants will understand.

'More people to be born and bred,
we give them goods, but they're not fed,
just a little so they work and breed,
for their money and their bodies we have a need,
and they'll need energy to live and thrive, for a while,
till the planet burns them alive.

We have technology on our side
and if you can afford it, you can hide,
for a while.
But as strange as it may seem
our structural society will have been a dream,
scientists now do us inform
that civilizational collapse will be the norm.

That means food production will slow and stop
people will begin to drop.

That's our kids we're talking about and theirs,
but by then all will have found out,
that the "Rights of Man" and "The Age of Reason",
was said wrong, it was 'The Age of Treason',
the treason against humanity against our 'human kind'.

We, the "herd", were 'befuddled and occupied' so we'd be blind.
This financial system now that rules the world of man,
has led to the 'Age of Treason' from companies that can
control the puppets that they place in power.
It just seemed like a choice
because of the manipulated media shower,
that rained down upon us into our mind and into our soul
and left people in want and need in a system built on greed,
'All for me and none for you', it was a creed that held all through.

They kill the speech of the common man
and silence dissent from our thought where they can,
and they can a lot, that's for sure,
they've treated the people like manure.

Which of course is how they think,
it's the poisoned chalice from which they drink.
Once you take a sip it orientates your mind,
until there's nothing left, no more good to find.
The problem is, it's like a bug and it's in the system – now – of how we live
and conduct our life,
it's incorporated into our education,
so much so, that all these seem the norm, abnormalities;
much that is horrific passes our way,
but we treat it as if it's normal life every day.

Violent films lead us to anaesthetize
our feelings before our very eyes;
we have a society built on violence and lies.

In the main people care, we really do,
but it's manipulated now through and through.

'Bombard their mind, confuse and distract,
divert their attention from basic fact;
we play this game so you think you can choose,
maybe you have a chance, but in the end you'll always lose.
We can kill you with a glance,
we have a stare and it's the 'Gorgon' one of old myth,
we'll freeze you or we'll appease you
till you can no longer move.
Life is a record; you're stuck in a groove,
and we know the tune to play, hell, we make you sing it every day'.

It's the track of old that's always new;
we give you something else to do,
we like the place you 'occupy',
we've always got something new to buy.
But here's the secret and here's the way,
if you stopped buying what we sell and say,
what could we do,
we'd have to share some of our riches with you.

But thankfully that will never get to be,
we manipulate it so that you buy all that you see,
and we package well, you can tell,
because even though many do suspect the truth,
that our house is made of paper and if you so choose,
you can blow down our roof.
But that will never be,
you've been silenced,
you just don't see.'

Human-kind – If only he could be

Some human tendencies have been exploited,
to produce a society left disjointed,
lop-sided in its feelings of care,
lost – wandering on a planet – going no-where.
Manipulated and induced – to love the self – we've been seduced.

This tendency has been strengthened
by those who wish to remain unmentioned,
for selfish power likes to work in the dark,
it keeps things damp, there's no spark
to light the flame that will cast a little light in humanity's true name –
'wise-man'.

Human-kind, if only he could be, wrapped up in all sorts of bonds and
invisible chains, trapped by the powers that speak in his name.
The tendencies of the human psyche that have been discovered and
abused and guided people into a world of selfish care,
leads to a lack of affection for others – out there.

'Love the Self' others are like you, they don't care,
so be the same, you'll get somewhere'.

This seems to be the way of the modern market place,
for a society that is taught that life is a race - to the top –
if you don't make it, you will drop,
you will be an under-achiever if you're not a 'self-love' believer.

We've had a couple of generations of this attitude without cessation;
it's now inherent in the system in which we live,
struggle for yourself, to others, nothing give,
is that the way you wish to be, your inner life dying silently,
to 'love the self' above all things, only tragedy does that bring.

If that is a primary and in control,
then love of yourself will sell your soul.
The society has no chance to survive,
for not enough people will strive,

to bring a balance back to the self, as a first; but for the planet it's a must,
that would take time and quite possibly way too much,
for the love of self is our crutch.

Once again, it's been embedded to be that way,
especially now, today.
It is incredible that energy companies are proud to boast and say, about
what they take from our ground, still, now, today,
and that it was said for another 100 years –
tell me, is it not clear that nature disappears?

The love of the self – 'self-love' – wants all the power – thinks nothing is
above, and in a way it has risen to the top,
and like a hungry predator it can't stop,
addicted to its important self, it's a psychological attitude of ill health.

So, the problem is 'attitude',
but now it leads to social control, manipulate the poor, the weak,
with their mind play hide and seek.
It may as well be called 'Jekyll and Hyde',
for the powerful have the double face, one on each side.

'Confuse and befuddle the numbed down public with a smile,
tell them what we do is all worthwhile,
while the other face controls their thought
and makes them happy with what they bought.

When they complain or dissent,
persuade them their money is well spent,
keep them under surveyed control, just in case they wake up,
and want to be whole.
We don't want them to rise above their station, place and class,
militarize the police, break up that mass,
but tell them that we care and we do it all for them,
and that democracy is always this way,

we have the gun so we always have the say.

So, be happy with what you got; we know it's not a lot,

but we love no-one more than us – all for me and none for you -
it's our creed, we thought you knew,
we love ourselves, what about you?
Are you catching on with what we do,
it took a while but it's worked quite fine,
all that was yours is now mine.'

Love me, (I do)…

*These men have a paper heart, it makes it easier to rip
apart, shredded just like our laws, evil done just because…
So, this is no love poem to God; that's why we give you a
paper heart, the real one's been shod.*

Cultured, yes, you have been

The 'culture of cruelty' comes from a human trait,
that's been cultured – let in the gate;
the door is open that seems our fate.
Humans, who should have known better,
followed their leader's rules to the letter.

'Sink down into your lower self;
don't worry about your inner health.
Don't believe all that stuff, about how you should not be rough,
with other beings or with what you're seeing.
Ignore what it is you feel, pretend it isn't real;
we can help you in that way, tell you things to sooth your day,
we give you drugs to make you forget, and take the pain away.

Some will say it will affect your soul, but there's no proof of that;
we need cattle for the slaughter,
we'll take your son or your daughter,
we'll let you breed, we have a need.

But as we breed you like a beast,
we must control your mind at least,
so that you do not begin to realize or suspect
that there's something you do not detect,
that you were born for a purpose higher than what we allow.

But even if some of you escape our chains,
we can survey all, we'll pull in the reigns,
and we'll guide you to where we want you to go,
we run this un-holy show.

We'll break you down, we'll keep you poor,
we'll quell dissent, we'll use you like manure.
You've got 100 trillion neural connections in your brain,
just like us, but we 'occupy' much of them with our new toys.
Ain't life a buzz?
Just in case you don't know how far we control this show? That's at least
1000 times the number of stars in our galaxy.

Common Sense

We spin around here out in space;
as you can tell it's a really large place;
but way down here on planet earth
we're in control and in charge, our ego's gotten rather large.
We have much of something called money,
we think it's rather funny,
and the more we have, the less you do,
and we've manipulated that through and through.

We need workers for our 'planet hive', just to keep us alive.
You are our workforce for our different farms;
and we have soldiers who respond to the alarms.
They control and survey all over, they put down any independent dissent
and call for a better way of life to be.
Until you die, we'll keep you working unceasingly,
and even as you get older every day,
we'll work you till you drop, with little pay.

With a hundred billion neurons in your brain,
sometimes you realise our game. So we must distract and deflect,
what it is that you detect,
that we that lead you, have no 'real being',
this is really what you're seeing.'

The Golden Rule

There is a Golden Rule which we try to follow every day.
We take many different paths in order to hide what we say,
but it's clear to all of those that can perceive
if they've woken up from what we tell them to believe.
'all for me and none for you',
it's the Golden Rule we have in all we do.

We've embedded it in your education and in your every thought
and want; it's in the form of greed to fill unnecessary needs.
We cultivated them to a fine degree, mostly through media and T.V.

You're sitting in a room with you and a box full of life's fantastic offerings that
we tell you that you want or need.
We occupy you with made up stories to embed a seed –
that will take root and grow in you, so that as you grow, it will too,
then you'll be in our consumer plot
and all you have, you will have bought.
That sends your riches onto us, we're at the top and in control of this lovely
tree, the one you call humanity.

We are powerful, rich and we have all,
we keep you down; you have to crawl,
you only see our shadow on a wall.
We play you like a puppet on a string;
we tell you – if you join our play - you too can have everything.

But we don't leave that to chance;
we infiltrate everything, even romance.
We play with your heart, tell you to marry, give a ring or two,
make it gold or diamond, it's good for you.
It stays with you till your end,
but it's too late now. You've spent your money my friend
and all the extras that are included in the play,
it costs a lot, but many do it every day.

Reform

What would reform mean for the human race?
It would mean consumerism would have to step back a pace,
it would change our social face, public transport would be renewed, to be
clean and cheap and then there's oil to be subdued.

Companies must adhere to a common law,
and they must not be held in awe
by our people in power who bow down before
and offer them an opening door
to retire and to join the political band,
for their business ways they understand.

To be told the truth and not immersed in lies,
food production to localize,
building cities in ways to cut down on energy and waste,
it's many sided that you see. We build with no future planning, with great
haste. The forests of our planet to replenish with a mass influx of growth,
solar and wind to be implemented on a Global scale, it's a matrix of complex
systems at work interacting one and all.
When we change one, we start to change all.
And all it needs is to begin.

Planetary Piracy is a Crime

It's a planetary emergency because it's a planetary piracy;
the 1% have robbed us whole,
for money and all it brings they sold their soul,
they may not think that they've been bought
for all they think they have got.

But they lead the world to this mess
where 99% have increasingly less.
The question is revolution or reform? They want no pressure to reform,
for to power, addicted is the norm.
So what about a revolution? Is that the only other solution?
Many deaths would come with that action of social change, transforming a
revolution of selfish thought from the world would be good; but they don't
see that they ever could.

Can the powerful be shaken? They will continue to media blitz and militarize
all they sell to us with their lies,
they will continue to occupy our mind and thought,
and with all-purpose surveillance, we'll all be caught.

It needs a revolution of the common man.
The 'Age of Reason' should be called the 'Age of Treason',
of humanity sold down the drain, into a life of deadly pain.
Most have been kept poor and often in the dark,
distracted by the media noise, spend your money, buy our toys.

These days of austerity and control
of a population alive but never whole,
people of the 99% want change and to dissent from the way they've been
told to be, because this way is not out of necessity.
If they do protest – they will be violently repressed.
It was a good idea to occupy – the rich it did annoy.

They feared it was close to revolution times. For a 100 years at least, the
'Age of Treason' is now here,
it holds humanity back in chains and in fear.
The problem though is now for all, the planet heats, humanity falls; species

extinction means one and all.

It would be great to have a reform,
of care and kindness as the living norm,
but into society now it has been bred,
care only for yourself and that you're fed,
don't bother about other beings, be self-conceited in the main,
think of only what you can gain.
It's a tendency that has come and been induced into the psyche of the
modern man. Do not do for others when in reality you can.

Masters of the Human Race

The 'other side' of looking at the light

When you look at the light, imagine it is looking at you; it's a way of sensing
yourself and becoming aware of what you do.
I hear in some cities now that that is what they do. Observation from above -
street lighting - could it be love - seeing everywhere you go, no stopping; it's
a 24-7-365 show.

That should make you uncomfortably aware - for a while -
on you the many eyes that stare.
With every step you take, every move you make, every purchase, every call,
it's now recorded, one and all.
What you write or say is now looked at every day.
There's a freedom that has gone astray.
There's a collective sadness, now, every day.

The sadness of the behaviour of those we did elect,
as to our lives, they were meant to protect,
not invade our body, mind and soul,
steal our privacy and chuck it down the "memory hole".

It's a power they now abuse; it's a power they should lose.
Eyes upon you everywhere, even just sitting on a stair.
Step into a shop and you are seen, your face, your telephone, everywhere
you've been. It's an amazing abuse of power and control; a population
observed completely whole,
nothing can escape this 'net'.

All governments seem now to apply this catch and capture of information -
just going by.

As the technological side does advance,
there is no-one that has a chance,
to live a life that is private and unseen.

Now we really have our 'technological dream'.
There are no laws adhered to or put in place
to keep a check on these 'masters of the human race'.

A spider's web of a tensegrity nature, touch one thread it pulls the other, with
acceptance we have relinquished our freedoms that have been vanquished.
It's been a frenzied attack on a 'human right';
it's out of control day or night.
Those 'masters' are delirious in their power and control a whole society -
body, mind and soul;
so remember all of this when you look at that light,
the one that stares back at you day or night.

In a way it could be fun; if you're ever lost, you don't need to run,
just log in and ask those that stare,
'excuse me, I don't know where I am, do you know where?'

If you walk into a shop and can't remember why you're there,
touch your phone and ask them your memory to repair.
They'll tell you what you're most likely to buy.
Phones will have an emotional empathy, it will first give a sigh,
so it will all seem as if it's doing you a favour
and with that cute little voice and smile upon your screen,
will take away that sour taste that you really savour.

Machines that make it easy for you to interact with someone you thought
you knew or didn't,
put on your glasses and they'll tell you what you need to know,
as you communicate and watch the screen show.

Meeting people in the street will be no more mystery;
you can simultaneously gaze upon their history.
It's there for you to see,
but you must remember - yours as well will be.

It wasn't so long ago that you thought a book was meant for you to know,
it was there waiting to be read,
at that right moment it entered your life, heart and head,

it influenced what you would think, made you take a different drink from the
cup of life. – Well, fewer books are bought today,
because all the information is on its way, travelling through space in no time
at all – suddenly it's in your mind.

We seem to have rather a great store of information at our door.
Doors of perception sadly this is not,
doors marked 'deception' may be what we bought.

Fun it may well be, body language courses before your very eyes;
what people do will be no surprise,
every gesture, every movement will be interpreted to increase your chances
of improvement, and if the machine gets it wrong,
well, it will play a soothing song
to lull you into sleep again, to help you analyse your best friends.

And societies social problems it can mend,
there's an 'app' just around the bend.

So once again it seems to be that there is light
at the end of the tunnel,
but it's still a speeding train that has a CO_2 funnel,
and no matter how fast we can be,
our planet counts time differently.

So get ready for the coming shock,
because about Global Warming 'They' don't talk;
it encroaches and in no time at all
you'll be up with your face against a wall.
That wall is nature and it doesn't take a break,
and it doesn't care that it's your life at stake.
As a population is kept subdued,
with total control and all things can be viewed,
it can be truly called - a tragedy.

Occupy the mass with trivia or survival. Public relations have no rival. Enjoy the show, because you've been played, you've been enslaved; it's 24-7-365, Global Warming burns everything alive.

It must be Fun - to be Rich

(Death – Destruction – Despair)

You know, it's probably fun to be rich,
just like it would be to be a witch or a warlock or a magician;
after all, you'd have to be a special kind of being
to give up all that power that you're seeing.

If you were rich would you give up your wealth,
if it only depends on another's health?
Would you give up the power to buy everything that you could try?

To buy big boats and fast cars, to pay for trips, even to Mars,
to give up power and control of other people down below,
to give up your money to understand
what it must be like to live off the land?
Maybe for a week or two, but not forever that wouldn't do.
All that power in your hands,
no, like a magician or a witch you'd want to stay simply rich.

There's no need to give up all, to help humanity not to fall,
but you could have your own rich movement,
to help us all with some improvement.
These charities that help are awfully nice,
but if they're tax deductible, you don't need to think twice.

Financing culture is very good, but a billion people have no food. You could
finance a culture of care – everywhere – you have the money,
you have the power and control,
one big effort, humanity could be whole.

So much money is spent on war
and no-one knows what they're fighting for.
A fraction of what is spent
would feed humanity without leaving a dent
in that 'cost' that goes to death, destruction and despair.

Come on and help – you have a real heart in there –
how about a special coalition of the rich and plenty,
one that gets together and redirects
the politicians who are not heartless and empty.

You could do it, you know you can. It's possible to be a human man.
The power from this will not come from your mind;
there are unintended consequences from humans
being partially blind.
Nothing goes in a straight path, sometimes we invoke the opposite,
it's like a wrath of a strange kind,
it's like travelling with your eyes shut, there's always a 'but'.

But, to cut a long story short, there are many things you could do,
and you know them too.
There is one generation left - after that our chance is gone. It needs a mass
movement. Why don't you join – bring some of that invested coin, talk to
others, increase you're social conscience standing?
Do it with love, don't be demanding.

If you do wake to this call, it will be for one and all.
Change the policy of war; no-one knows what they're fighting for.
You can save the poor and underprivileged of our world,
it's possible. Treat yourself to 'austerity'.
Stop the governments destroying human rights,
help in humanity's darkest night.
You too can bring a light, and bring a balance back,
cease this worldwide attack that will lead to a Global Warming end.
All will not be well, this your heart does tell.

R I C H

Regularly Increasing Capital Handsomel

INNER SENSE

Perceptions from within

Pre-poem - Emotions Vs Intellect

Pre-poem - Emotions vs Intellect

Perhaps the battle is not real, about what you think or feel. Illusions come from both these sides of man; it blocks us – like a small perception only can. Religion and science must co-join in our day, acceptance and tolerance, both have a say.

Different ways of perceiving truth, it's limited anyway – so let's raise the roof. Perhaps we can comprehend just a little more before Global Warming closes our door.

War of Words

In the war upon our world it's hard for people to see or sense the idea of goodness, of purpose beyond survival. We are being bombarded with ideas that teach the "selfie" has no rival.

Those that are prone to love their mind often seem to be spiritually blind, as if it's stupid to consider life as sacred, as if it's a base and lower thought - something that can emotionally be bought.

And yet, often, if you look upon their hand there's a wedding ring that represents a sacred band. And if you asked about what's closest to their heart, it would be their wife and children - they don't want to part.

When you hear the intellectual talk, the world and its wonders are dissected into pieces analysed and prized, always talking about the design of the structure they observe, and talking of the conforming of the laws of nature with reserve. They leave out the idea of what created them in the first place, as if human or any other form of life was an accident, just on this little place called Earth.

Emotions never seem to enter the equation, despite the fact, people's intellectual attitudes are governed by what they like or dislike, which has emotional content at its base. Our pre-conscious actions may be governed by our unseen but felt emotional mess.

A scientific point of view is that the observer interferes with what he sees at the moment of observation. An interesting point of view when looking at "pre-conscious actions": In the self – if we are ruled – controlled – pre-set by what we like or dislike, then the stage is set for the play and it's our emotions of habituated associations 'like or dislike' that may get in the way.

And if this attitude of thoughts gets stronger as it goes along then this point of view only grows strong – attached to a habitual emotional thought, it becomes our forget-me knot.

One idea that scientists mostly agree, that life, all life, is made rather intelligently. There's no accident in these varied endless designs; it's pretty structured where it's analysed fine. But something that seems to be difficult to believe is that we are made by a higher intelligence, just because 'that' we can't perceive.

In a world of seven billion beings, many follow teachings of which there are no external 'seeing's', they're ruled by what they feel. The 'intellectual' thinks that isn't real. But in this day and 'Age of Change' that may be a mistake, for all life on Earth is at stake.

To consider things from the other area of reaction, the emotional is for many a big attraction. Different religions have their own teachings and their ways, some of those will be extreme in their days. But in general, it's an emotional feeling and approach to the question "Who am I?" "Why am I here?" "What is the purpose of human life or life at all at its base?" – It's a scientific question but with an emotional face.

It's being simply asked in a different way; so perhaps, it should not be put down from an intellectual say; it's no more nor no less than the same question "What is life and what am I?" In these days of needs, where people's needs must co-join, a tolerance of other's belief systems could be the common coin.

It's a simple idea – separate we die – together we can try, to change our ways. There is no doubt what our scientists have found out. Our kids and theirs will live in warming days, many will not survive, later they will burn alive. To deny this is simply to turn away from what your children will live through in their coming days.

We've fixed ourselves in a system of continual decay, where we want new things - almost every-day, tied into a helter skelter sliding faster at the end. It's an 'imminent climate world crises', reality T.V. just around the bend.

The scientists of different branches of knowledge that we have must co-join with the billions of people who believe in 'something' not visible to perceive. All religions are obviously from the past and their purpose may have them outrun at last. This may or may not be the case, it doesn't matter anymore, it's a Global Warming in all of humanity's face.

There was an idea that religion could hold man near the spiritual side – the unseen, the missing essential key of his complexity. But for our reality now, it makes no difference what your mind has bought, whether you agree with religions or not. Nature has no straight lines; everything loses power or deviates after a while. Institutions, religions or economies are no exceptions to this natural law; in our modern world we seem to have lost the sense of sacred awe.

We need to begin the 'Age of Change', our opportunity moves out of range. Controllers of might, of power lead our world to this planetary death. They make these laws, they keep control, and seven billion of us lose our soul.

Ideas connect to give us purpose. We need the emotions to join for their energy surplus, which we need on a massive scale; otherwise humanity will fail. Only individual and collective emotions will give us this human directive, and it could direct us to where we have to go. Democratic world socialism – the only world left to know.

We've been distracted by petty things, it's in our system, it's what it brings. Change the system, change the laws, we have no better cause; we need new Global Warming Laws.

The Call of Being

Do you have a sense that something's wrong? That something is not where it belongs? A sense of sadness, as if something is lost, or almost gone; a sense of it is there - but you just can't put your finger on? There is a call on 'Being' - on what you will receive may depend on what you believe – there is a call on 'Being' but this you may not be seeing.

On what you love or give your attention to, may well be your God for you. This is not about religion, this is about the inner life of man, it's about 'something' that we were meant to feel, if we ever can. Not for all that seems sure. In our societies we are educated to treat others like manure, others of another race, another colour, another belief system, another mother. When they're not your blood and not your own, what is it that you are shown?

Where is your inner life and outer concern? Survival takes us mostly, this we learn; but there is a call, a call on Being, a Being to become aware.

II

The events of life distract us, this is meant to be so, it's how the rules are set, dispensed down below. The Call of Being is to gather and collect – ourselves – individually, apart; awareness, a dying art. As paradoxical as it seems, sometimes we're aware of a world where we live in our dreams. This is something we all feel, it's like raising your head above the water and air to drink; but we all fall back down into the 'waters of forgetfulness' and there we sometimes swim, but mostly we sink.

'The Call of Being' is to make us think, think about our state, because it's not too late, the call is always there, it's never stopped, it's never gone away, it's just the river rose higher, so that we forgot ourselves in there.

This state of 'things' did not need any help, it happens all the time. Life is designed this way; man may never be fine. That's man's choice, but for that he needs to hear 'The Call of Being' of being aware, and this is something – for a multitude of reasons – man seldom does. Man may not need any help to be immersed in his daily woes and dreams, but these days, sadly, we have a mass of it, it seems.

There is no doubt we are taken by the media society that has come about. As a parent you will feel it, see it, in your kids; they get so easily lost in modern media and its pulls; but then, see and accept that we're just older fools, distracted from ourselves and attracted to sleep inducing pastimes, and yes, they become past-times and present times all the time.

There's no holding the moment, there's no being aware, there's nobody going anywhere. And on a speed heating planet that runs out of time, we have controllers in charge who are not leading for the human good, when we need leaders that really should. 'Controllers of policy', 'controllers of deals', work wheels within wheels. It's confusion for the common man, especially if they are distracted from doing anything they can – to save our world.

The distractions have been multiplied and magnified, these endless policies of control for power, this is a tornado, a tsunami, it's not a shower and it rains down upon the common man. It's a blame society and 'they' blame us the 99% all 'they' can. 'Pass the buck, make them feel it's their fault they're out of luck.'

Well, it's not our fault; we don't lead, we let you be in charge; you make us and our planet bleed. But what's really sad and terrible is that you implement policies that take man down to the barbarous state. Millions all over the world die. You call it our fate, sure, as in fatal. But it was not and is not the only way to be. This attitude of dominance and control which at its very base is VIOLENCE – you are violent to the rest of humankind and sadly you don't seem to mind. This is sociopathic and you're happy to be that way, where you lead the world and you have the say.

The pawns that are placed in charge, the ministers of laws and rules of our countries bow down before you on bended knee, they treat you like the king of all to be, you are masters, they and we are slaves, they get benefits and a higher rate of pay.

The call to be has gone silent with so much distractions and policies that are selfish and VIOLENT. It takes a lot of power to silence seven billion beings. A lot of influences that are evil in intent is really what we are seeing, it's power that has gone astray and it's a power that is gaining day by day; but eventually there will be 'The Swing of the Pendulum'.

The progression and self-education of mankind cannot go forever on;

there is always an opposite of every swing of the pendulum. It may depend upon what man is based upon. 'The Call of Being', the call of the lower or the higher self, but you could also say the inner or more outer man, will depend upon what a man can; these levels are in every man.

There are no exceptions to this rule, it's just we don't always listen to this 'tool'. Tool can be the right word to use, but a tool like any other we can abuse, for some there will be a magnetic pull, for others, for most of life. They'll just play the fool, forgetting that embedded quality and possibility that came with them when they were born.

We all must grow up into the society fate takes us to, where we are, the parents, the family. We need the basic education, the surroundings of where we be. But there is a pull, silently; it pulls you back to become aware, that there is more to life than what you see - out there, with your senses.

Man has a special possibility, he can be aware, of the inner and the outer, simultaneously. But this is not something that happens accidently; no, this must be cultivated, and this wish must grow, otherwise, yes, all the world is a stage, but you don't own the show, you will just be an actor playing your part every day, every day, every day, the scenery may change but the same script you will say.

The life of the habitual self, we all know that's true, is not difficult to see, it's just we accept and fall down internally. We go back to sleep and live the life of the waking dream. A life that knows it's living, it may never have been.

Only you can tell that, do you live the lie? It's not an intellectual concept but intelligent you must be; it's about awakening inside about what you need to see, 'The Call of Being'.

What do we need? What must we be? We have a world that's heating rapidly. We don't see it day by day – in general it's beyond our sense capacity. So it's never on the top list of survival – but humankind has never had such a rival.

Of course there is a close second lurking in the shadow of man, the nuclear time-clock; it's moved 3 minutes to midnight but not the closest it can. It's amazing that we even have a table for that to be able to threaten to obliterate the existence of all you see. What type of "leaders" rule our world for that to be? Not leaders of being that's for sure, that's not what we're

134

seeing.

Businessmen shouldn't be running the world, they've made a mistake; it's clear for all, it always has been. Power corrupts and this is what we're seeing, and unfortunately, this is what we have to live with and deal with or die with. There are many types of death. But when you kill the inherent goodness in people this can be truly called an 'Evil'; if you're really religious then it would be a sin.

Violence is in our society, in the culture of man; this we know, any thought if you feed it can grow. The problem is, today we're taught to feed these thoughts. It's good for business and war to educate our kids in violent games, it's good for business to increase the violence in films and make it much the same.

It's good for business to call other people names, especially of another colour, another race, even just another mother. Negativity or fear in any form is good for business. It's good for control; it gives those that lead a race of beings whole. Multiple methods of attraction and distraction guide humanity round this 'merry go round', and there's nothing merry about it.

It's good for business to manipulate the inner life and call of man, to confuse and distract with anything you can; it's really good for business if people watch T.V. every day and see the latest movie that gets sent their way. It plays on their emotions and traps them in their dreams, "Give them Heroes to aspire to, they know what it means."

The consumer plot, excellent what a trick that was brought into the life of man. Anything is good for business, it seems, religions, marriage, war, poverty, hope, envy, desire and a matrix of other emotions that feed the fire.

The Fire that Burns

Sure, our planet heats, that could be looked on as a fire. Sure, nuclear war is a closer reality than it's ever been due to the types of leaders that lead our world, that have seized control, with laws and violence and mental and emotional manipulation. These things are sure. But there is another fire, the fire that burns in all people everywhere, the fire for the wish to be. The call of being, of becoming, what humans were meant to be.

That feeling is not atrophied in humans yet, but it is subdued, or it's consciously or unconsciously misplaced, misdirected and in these days of induced Austerity suffering, combined with media distractions and manipulations, it's being abused, by people who don't emotionally realise the effects of what they do. They have internalized their actions; it's part of a slow indoctrination all through time.

The embers of this fire still burn in all people. There is evil and with seven billion beings, yes, there will be evil people, ruled by their lowest part; but these are the exceptions, not the rule. Mostly people just suffer or sleep in this mess we call society.

It's been a while since Mr Plato said these words, "We need teachers of being", and no doubt there were some. The cultivation of humanity, of civilizations depends on those people; it's the 'balancer' against the forces of barbarism that always knock on the door.

Originally, all real religions contained Teachers of Being, people who taught new ways to think about life and its meanings, with different but connected methods each time. The underground river of 'teachers of being' rising up at certain moments in human history, needing to preserve what had been achieved until then, in order to begin a new age once again, when the swing of the pendulum started to move away from the barbarous actions that leave nothing but destruction in their wake.

This underground river of 'teachers of being' slowly penetrates in order to give a new impulse, a new way, a new method, a new approach to this high aim, which, like all other things, deviate from its original intention, and purpose, needed and adapted for the new times people live in. These people enter human history and bring a new age, an age of change. Through history these changes took decades, if not hundreds of years, the power of their ideas weakening and becoming distorted naturally, from what they were meant to be or where they were meant to lead.

These people are historically known to be teachers to billions the world over; they taught different approaches to the same end and emphasized different aspects probably depending on necessity. Therefore we have the same but different. Let's cut through time and come to the now, this Age of Change; and an Age of Change it must become, or it will be forced upon us in the coming climate change of our world.

What do we need for a successful 'Age of Change'?

Unfortunately, so many things that I couldn't list them and don't know them all anyway. There are many people who write about the practical realities needed to save humankind. And this information these days becomes quickly dispersed amongst the peoples of the world. From protests and making connections from leaving oil in the ground to ceasing wars of domination and control or to turning away from capitalism combined with raising the minimum wage, saving the coral reefs, systems of the world and so on.

There are so many possibilities. People are attracted to and work with what takes them or what is possible for them. So let's take a look at it from another point of view, due to all the previously mentioned attractions and distractions working on all people everywhere.

There is a lack of emotional reality, the lack of an imminent feeling of danger. We're not in 'fight or flight' mode, the survival mechanism hasn't kicked in yet, for when that happens on a personal level; you're on edge all the time.

The mental appreciation of the fact is there for the many and for them they will feel a personal connection with that, the emotional perception of truth. And of course some of these writers try to write in such a way that affects others into some form of action, the 'butterfly effect'; it has to be that way, but let's connect all this to what this paper is about, 'The Call of Being'.

For that, we need the energy of certain emotions, not anger, despair, hopelessness and so on, but the energy of a contained awareness and recognition of our situation, a developing awareness of this sad ending to humankind and in reality to organic life on Earth. It truly may be looked upon as having a wild party in a big mansion with all the masters and slaves inside, in a state of business as usual. Some of the slaves are running around seeing the reality of the coming danger, trying to raise the alarm and being dismissed by the masters. The party's on 24-7-365, it's loud, there's lots of entertainment, lots of amusing distractions; but the fire's approaching, it's in the grounds. The slaves want to take care of the fire, but the masters, being so absorbed with their sense of self-importance, self-worth, self-power and position are also educated to enjoy the party life, they insist it won't affect them, at least not today or in their lifetime; other generations will have to deal with the problem. So what do the slaves do... you finish the story...

The Call of Being

The call on our being would be a call to lead us to be something we are obviously not. We all know by now our leaders can't lead us there; they lack that personal development and quality of real empathy and compassion. Those qualities are not in the job description act; there isn't a section on the application paper. So not being a caring person is part of the occupational hazard of the profession they're in, making money, business, capital, when working for those aspects of our society, emotional qualities of care and compassion don't come along, sadly; life becomes a game and people become players learning how to manipulate all the rules of the game to disastrous outcomes for all of the other non-players.

All that may be so, it may be true, but what do we need?

We need a more caring society.

So, how do we get there?

Through mass change in education: our aim must be to reduce carbon emissions, keep the oil in the ground, stem and put a stop on the causes of that type of exploitation in the first place which come from the basic tendencies and inadequacies of capitalism and its inherent connections within our societies. Power - individual control in the hands of the few, has lead us here, with privatization of education, the prison system, healthcare, the militarization of the police force, patriarchy, racism, sexism, slavery in bondage or in economic austerity policies. Destruction of our eco systems of balances, wars of domination and control, unfortunately, the list is seemingly endless, it's a helluva lot of interconnected threads of the web of this human induced deceit, served upon us by the masters and makers of policy.

One has to admit that many people in our world have no interest or are unwilling to give time to this subject. But there are and always have been people interested and are pro-active in their thoughts, wishes and actions. Throughout the world there are pockets of people, unfortunately poor and unconnected and marginalized to the outer edges of general discourse.

Why so much emphasis on media manipulation?

Because every form of media, T.V. shows, ads, films, almost everything absorbs our attention, time and energy; it subdues people and puts them to sleep. Of course it must be acknowledged that anything and everything can put you to sleep. Most things that absorb our interest put us to sleep; by sleep is meant that we lose conscious awareness of ourselves: an awareness that is concerned with sensing and being mindful at the same time. Obviously that can be taken from you by your very own thoughts and usually is; we don't need media to fill that role. It's in all mankind's history, in a sense, that may well be our curse.

Probably the most accurate definition of its opposite would be being mindful, with what we do, in our daily actions. It's difficult to define accurately, there are so many definitions. And strangely enough there are often more terms for the opposite of being identified, lost, taken; the search for the opposite is usually found in religious or spiritual teachings.

Phrases like, being aware, mindfulness, attention, not forgetting, different forms on non-doing, non-end gaining, these words and many others all leading to the idea of being more present - more living in the moment, now. Connected with the idea of being aware, is the idea that people presume it's a quality that they already have, because their eyes are open and are aware a little of what they sense or see, where they are, how they feel. It's a very large and wide subject, thousands of books are written on it. Its big business these days, seven billion beings on a planet, there must be a helluva lot of them that feel lost and are magnetically attracted to those ideas.

Nearly three billion live in poverty and have limited modern education, so depending on their birth circumstances, different religions will interest them. Despite the fact that all religions lose their initial force and impulse through passing time, there is still that magnetic pull in people that will draw them towards whatever religion they are born into. Of course many these days rebel against that and deny the existence of a higher meaning or try a different religion thinking they were meant for another way and that the one they were born into does not suit them.

So can media be regarded like the modern religion?

No, not really, it's more like modern opium. It puts people into passive states, indulging in fantasies, hypnotized by the play before their eyes. They, we, you, me, all become actors in our own play, and the play is not only in "all the world's a stage", it's the play of your mind and the stage of your being. We live and often sleep through the drama of our own life, but it seems more appropriate to use the ancient Greek idea, it's a 'tragedy': which is pretty appropriate for that particular country and its people at the moment.

Lost, taken by anything and everything, religions and certain teachings essentially try to bring people back to that sense of presence that is missing so much today in the modern man.

Of course, a clear understanding of these various ideas becomes distorted through mis-understanding, personal interpretations, used by seekers of power instead of truth. So we are left with the mess we have today.

None the less, these are times we live in and we must make do. We must deal all with the necessities of this moment now. A planet of seven billion beings; and billions of us living in dire circumstances in regards to achieving any peaceful meditating moments. And others who don't live in war torn areas of our world and have enough food for survival are being deliberately immersed in the illusionary world of media, from the moment they can walk and talk till the moment they stop. So I can't think of a more appropriate word than 'Tragedy'; with all of the actions and events of survival occupying that quality once called sacred – attention. All that, while according to our scientists, the planet heats quicker than it's ever done before, another tragedy.

How do we activate an emotion strong enough to affect an 'Age of Change'?

Developing empathy enough to recognize that we must have compassion for those many increasing numbers of refugees fleeing from the wars raging across the planet, whether it's war-torn refugees or climate refugees or the austerity afflicted, that would be a good beginning: along with many other things.

Being aware enough so that when you look at young people, blissfully unaware of what's happening and being not properly informed about what's coming towards them like a speeding train – to recognize for yourself that it's being maintained that way. So, to organize, to speak, to spread and bring awareness of this situation and to help people escape from this sense of complicity that is embedded in our culture in many forms.

In a short and adequate formulation: we need the power of awareness, rage and sorrow. When we look at people we don't keep in mind that they will die and we don't hold that thought; it's not a great thought to hold, so it's understandable, but if we did, this would produce the power of an emotional empathy strong enough to affect an age of change.

'To be or not to be'

is the realization

'I am or I am not'

- for what you have, you have bought -

We can say it's not your fault, that you have been sold,
you have been told to believe that it's true;
but to wake up to this is something new.
And if it eats you from within,
then to ignore it becomes our sin,
for that would mean we ignore the mark,
and we'll never light the spark,
that must become a flame for it to burn.
To this calling we should return.

Humanity had its time to play,
but now its time runs out every day.
There's a shadow we have cast, it's the flag upon the mast,
it seems a pirate flag - it could well be,
everything's been privatized, isn't that planet piracy?
And isn't piracy a crime?

But what a scale and a path that has been taken – Human-kind has been
forsaken – led into the path of the inane; it's left us unbalanced, some say
insane.

Our path is suicide on a planetary scale;
as this ship is and continues; it will fail.
Pirates are at the helm and guide into the effects of climate change,
they hold us in the depths, trapped in chains.
These chains are like invisible threads,
because they're connected into our heads.
So we behave like puppets on a string;
they can literary tell us anything.

They had a 'Responsibility to Protect',
everybody feels it, your inner sense of right can detect.

But we've been guided away from what we should be.
That man who wrote those words "To be or not to be",
seemed to pose a question, when in fact it was a realization.

That "I am or I am not'
it just depends on whether my attention has been bought,
which can be so easily done,
there's nothing easier under the sun.
It's an ancient problem, right up till today,
all teachings talk about it in some way.

The key is awareness, many have that taught,
and it's something that if you want, cannot be bought,
though it can be taken from you, in any passing moment, we're susceptible,
that's how we've been made, but we have another option, we have another
choice.
But you have to look inside to hear that almost silent voice.
It doesn't rage or shout, all it says to you is the lights are on, but you're not
home, you're out,
it's whispering ever so gently in your ear, wake up my dear.

It doesn't tell you that you're bad;
as a matter of fact, that voice sounds rather sad,
for you ignore it time and again. Imagine it was your best friend.
It's there wherever you may go,
as if it's above and watching what you do in life's show.
You need to be silent for it to hear,
but if you are, it's always near.
When you get lost in what you do,
that voice or presence just seems to disappear, but remember,
you can call it back –
and once again it will be near.

To begin, it needs your thought to become aware,
send your attention into your body like a torch shining in the dark,
it ignites and lights the spark,
and it's necessary time and again,
if you want your spark to become a flame,

because it's the fire that you burn
if you want that voice to return,
you need to let it know you're there
ready and waiting, if you dare.

These simple words make a rhyme
but attention is of a vibration that is infinitely 'more fine',
finer than what we can behold,
if you're to believe what you've been told,
for the ancients say it's like turning lead into Gold.

Multiplicity

I am 'many times' it seems

Psychology of the modern age, which has been for many years all the rage,
(if you could afford it)
teaches a fundamental, not often under scrutiny,
that 'Man' has many 'self's'.

We look on this from different views that change
with flavour depending on what your inner does savour.
The 'Wild man' in you trapped in the modern shoe,
the 'Fool' an archetype of modern rule,
are just a couple to connect, to get your thought to suspect.

Anciently said, one type was a 'Tramp' who only made camp
and no deeper roots to sow, some of them you know
and that many may be 'Lunatic',
it's a strange idea that makes them tick.
There are others of course but there we do not need to go,
this little rhyme is simply to open up the show,
to highlight the irresponsibility of those in charge, who cannot be? For their
own house is not in order,
and this of course they do not see.

A 'Human Being' perhaps they will never be,
for deep inside they fail to touch or feel
as they cause death needlessly.
If you cause something, then you are the instrument through which that is
done. And if that is death, destruction, poverty or even inequality, then
there's no place left to run.

Stuck within the causes of your making, you live the life that you've been
faking, but it's not your fault; people are never taught how 'to be' which
means to face their own reality.

"The unreal has no being and the real never ceases to be."
We have a state of being-less leaders, unable to see.

The leaders lead, leading us over the 'climatic' cliff, lemmings on the run
whether we be brown, white, black, yellow, red or any shade of mixing,
we'll all be together dead.
As our increasingly warming planet becomes unsustainable for human life,
species extinction is only a matter of time;
it's 1,000 a week at the moment of this rhyme.

The Law of the Selfie

The law of the selfie has been induced and penetrated into the soul of man – a clever trick in a way, occupied with your 'self' every day. Like a child responding to that inner need in man, 'Hi, dad, look at me and what I can.' Or 'I'm unique, I'm different from others, in many a way. You can tell by how many clicks I get every day.' Of course, the capturing of a living moment on camera is also of emotional importance for many.

These and many other thoughts that penetrate into the soul of man, show myself as better than what I am. Social media, self-occupation, living in the cyber world without real sensation of who it is we really are, each generation has its own idea of the new cool; but often we remember and look back and think, what a fool.

Selfie

We seem to live through different ages; we supposedly had the 'Age of Reason'. Where we meant to be reasonable, when science came back into consideration? Seemingly the last time was when Pythagoras walked the ancient Greek streets, in a society where science and religion were meant to be one, an undivided study, two sides of the same coin, so to speak.

After the 'Age of Darkness' fell down upon the world, the times when religious persecution was at its height and possibly religious understanding at its lowest, came the 'Age of Reason'. It could have been named the 'Age of Treason'. The 'Treason of Man', all through those times there were different financial systems being tried out, capitalism won the day, and of course it still rules with its unfortunate side effects: capital accumulation for the few, poverty for the many. But the underlying problem in this system is that with capital accumulation comes financial, then political power of rules and laws over the masses, leading to poverty at home and wars of resources in other lands, all inflicting pain on billions of people through domination, destruction and death.

As the rich get richer, the poor suffer, with slow indoctrination over the ages of 'you too can rise in this system, if you work hard.' With the implication of be selfish, don't think of what your actions do to others, that you will never see. An appropriate saying expresses that, 'out of sight, out of mind' - one could easily add to that out of heart.

As well as all of the above mentioned horrors unleashed on the population of our planet, due to uncaring policies, there are the accumulated effects of carbon emissions by man, called these days, 'anthropogenic induced global warming'.

Carbon emissions, our output magnified in the last 25 years, takes us to the tipping point and soon over the edge where it would be impossible for human and many forms of organic life to survive.

Scientists tell us there is a generation of time left to try to slow the speeding train down that we most definitely are on. If not, then it's a couple of generations of increasing climate changes, which will devastate all life, destroying food production and eventually leading to civilization collapse: leaving a HOT world with no organic life.

Today, when personal awareness is very much at its lowest, we become lost and occupied by trivia and are induced and educated to think that this is a great idea. We try to capture these times of what should be a self-awareness moment, with a 'selfie', the modern expression of a captured celluloid time-shot.

The picture is there, the image, when you look at it later, there's no other sense induced; you' are simply looking at a picture of your lost self. If your other senses were involved and a deeper connection with your mind and emotions were there, perhaps you wouldn't have even raised the camera. A captured moment, but in reality a lost moment frozen in time, lost from the connection to the real self.

What about an internal Selfie?

It's been said by some that what humanity needs is a renewed or a change in spiritual awakening, difficult in the present world of concern with the selfie; in half the world with financial survival and in the other half with physical survival: but none the less.

Is it possible to take these selfies in the mind, to have and cultivate these moments of awareness, for that's what that is, you being aware of you in your surrounds, sensing yourself, aware of where you are, what or who is around you in space, aware of the internal speech or its play in the mind? The constant thoughts, the judgements and the unceasing commentary which may be often negative in character, running through the mind, awareness of all that - plus - an awareness of 'something else', that ('something' that) is almost always missing in our daily life - the sense of the miraculous.

That feeling of the miraculous formulated in so many ways, in different times in different teachings, often highlights only one or two aspects of a complexity, simple yet profound and often only coming with a magnetic pulling towards a sense of the sacred.

In some, the power of that pull will be strong, but if that magnetic pull is not sitting aright, it can lead to strange ways. Sometimes we worship strange Gods. In others, that pull will not be there, it has become weak and faded from many reasons. What they love, will be their God, what they give their time to, inner or outer, they will worship; we seem to love the God of the self above all other things. And what strange things we worship, some people love power, some food, some sex, some sport, some simply love chocolate. Some people love to be negative, some simply love their 'self', we look in the mirror, 'yes, the picture's okay.' We have an argument, 'Yes, I'm right,' "What strange beings that we are, that we worship ourselves."

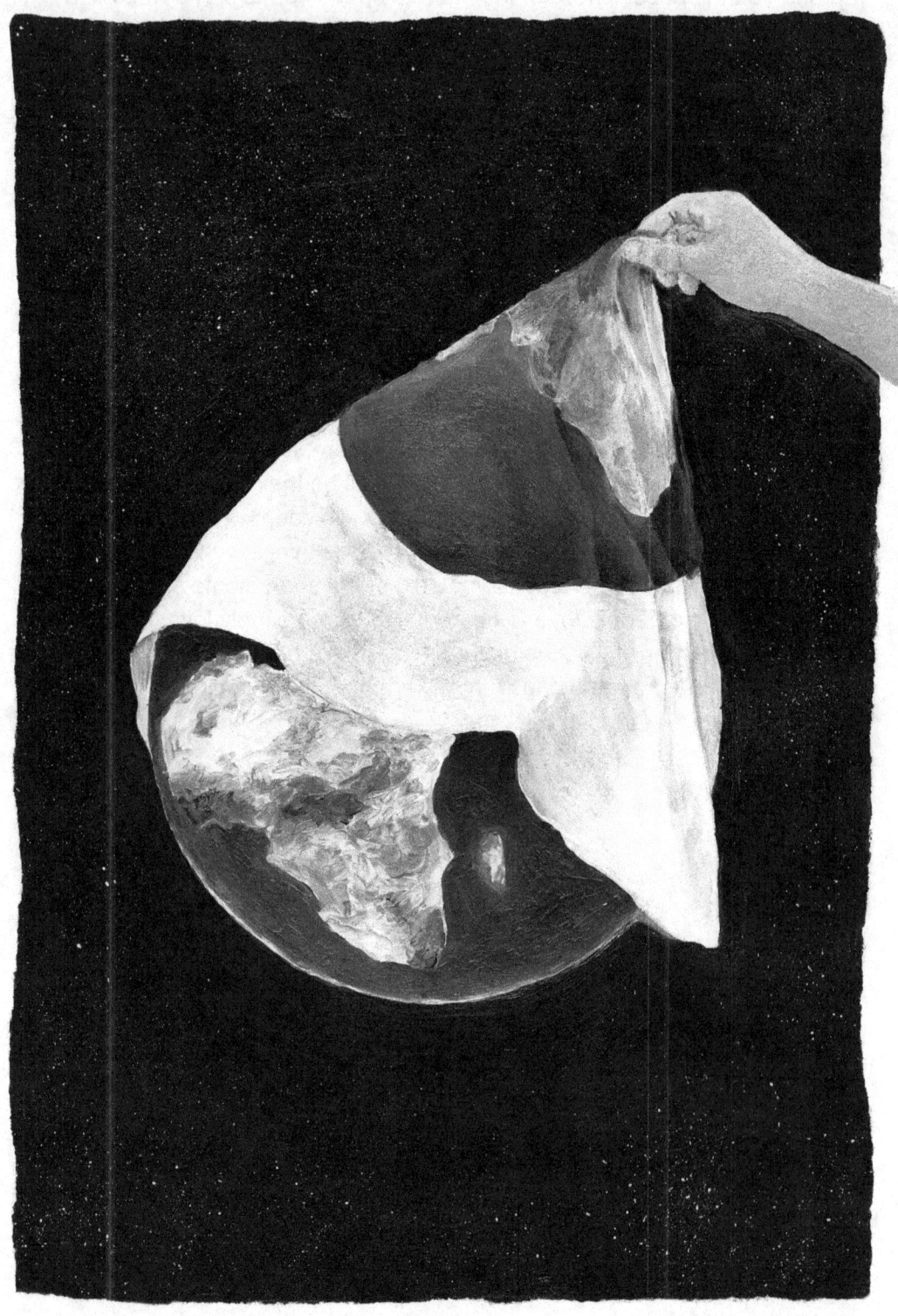

Sky-Truth

Being unveiled for what we are

The clouds in the sky are often one above the other,
the grey ones down below bringing rain, wind and storm;
but once you pass upwards there a little more,
it's plain to see there are no winds and storms above a certain height; and
what goes on down below just seems like a show
for you to observe.

Now to cut through that moment that you sense,
with it not to dispense,
as this book's about the coming Global Heat
and all things connected that won't be sweet,
you all know nothing survives above a certain temperature,
it's just a matter of Time.

Time seems to be a strange phenomenon doesn't it? Different life forms
live in their own time-lines or circles. All existing simultaneously as if they
are the wheels in an old fashioned watch, all moving at their own speeds.
Our ability to think and accept seems to be limited there, 'Doors of
Deception' rather than 'Doors of Perception'.

Still, it seems to be part of the experiences and events of being
human; perhaps not all things are meant to be understood, but instead to
evoke in us a sense of wonder. That wonder that we all had when we were
young, do you remember that, that sense of the inexhaustibly of everything,
then we start to acquire the things we need for survival, depending on the
society we're born into.

We all have our own story and unfortunately some poor souls only
have a short story, and don't survive very long. Some stories are
horrendous, and if we could truly feel them, would shock our sense of being.
We became occupied with things, usually ourselves in relation to things, but
taken, that's for sure; our attention was stolen like a thief that comes in the

night. Occasionally we find it again but lose it so easily.

Are we to blame for that? I don't know. I don't think so, it seems to be designed that way, we didn't have much of a say, but when certain things or moments touch you to your core or stop you in daily life and hold you there, aware, some things may take your breath away, some may cause you deep sadness or regret, some may cause you to question the meaning of life, your life in particular, some may cause you to feel there is no meaning to life.

But it would be a strange thing to have all these experiences there waiting for you, in existence already to come to, if there were no life waiting to be lived, waiting for you to come to these moments.

Each story must have its own experiences, its own ups and downs, characters, events, its own meaning, waiting to be lived. Some poor stories never have a chance, some are just imagination or romance, some live the helter skelter of life; and finally, we never really know where our own story will take us.

Then there's the human story, the human play

The subduing of most of the characters in the human play of life on planet earth by a few of the dominant actors, cause much suffering and death to the many for the sake of the few, and as a side effect burning our house down where our play is performed.

If there is a director of the human play, it seems he either left or got fired. Some actors feel he sometimes left a few general instructions written down with a few trusted actors about how to continue. As time passed these ideas were followed for a while, but as the stage turned many times over the years and the actors all changed, these different instructions were sometimes mis-interpreted, misunderstood, taken advantage of for selfish reasons, abused, some thought they were just general guidelines to follow occasionally, if it suited.

Others didn't believe that there were any real instructions or that there was ever a real director, they believe that they just appeared on the stage of life from nowhere.

Breathing, sensing, aware or unaware,
a complicated organism of life
and then, when they stop breathing, they go back to nowhere.
All in all it seems like a pretty confusing and sad play,
with much suffering and cruelty played out on it every day.

Others didn't believe that there were any real instructions or that there was ever a real director, they believe that they just appeared on the stage of life from nowhere.

Breathing sensing, aware or unaware,
a complicated organism of life
and then when they stop breathing they go back to nowhere.
All in all it seems like a pretty confusing and sad play,
with much suffering and cruelty played out on it every day.

It there's a director, then maybe the director's just waiting for it to run its course and begin a new one. Who knows? But it also seems that where there is no meaning, no feeling of a higher or deeper purpose, then people gradually gravitate toward self-interest or cruel and destructive tendencies, tendencies that lie dormant and waiting to takeover, in the end leading towards barbarism. Our limited view of history shows that degeneration of cultures go that way. Violence rules some epochs until some order is restored, until a balance is brought back.

As we have been told by our experts, that the house is becoming unsafe to live in and if we don't try to repair it soon, we won't be able to, they say it's not complicated, it's maths, but time runs out.

So it seems, we, the actors in our own play must redefine what role we have to fulfil. Also it seems we must have a meeting of a common cause to restructure how we live and remake our laws, to try to turn the heating down before the house blows up in our face and tumbles down. It's a small window of opportunity before the curtain starts the certain but definite dropping of its veil.

Is History Time?

It seems to be that there are two histories that run through time,
the history of progression and the history of crime.
The one of crime is the normal one we learn
and the story of progressive connectedness
is the one some people try to discern.

The one that can lead to the meaning of life,
a self-evolving organism comes to lots of strife.
We're given the power of our mind to use; the blind did abuse.

History of crime seems to affect the moral compass of those in power
and who laird their rules upon the peoples of planet Earth
with a shower of self-seeking wealth.

A social spiritual-ness would be lovely if it were so; unfortunately the so
called 1% leaves us struggling down below.
They themselves are trapped within their towers of wealth,
rich in possessions, and poor in inner health.
Of course they can have all things that money brings
but only to the tune that money sings
and a moderation of strife.
It's a struggle for the wish to be,
but the struggle's the same for you, for me.

Whether you be rich in goods, or poor and in debt
we all struggle with life's acts; many help others on their way,
it happens every day.

But also negativity often rules our daily life, a word, a look, an act,
gone in a moment of unthinking;
for we forget, what river of life from which we had been drinking.

The ancients tell us: two rivers flow,
it's a case of in which one do we go, two rivers, two histories of humankind,
one is aware, one is blind,
one is kindness, one is crime.
Sadly, they seem to struggle in this thing we call 'Time'.

Thus the struggle to simply be is not always easy for you
or me. One river may pull your inner heart,
but the other is hard from to depart.

Religions have served their purpose through time
to keep something spiritual in humans that's fine.
But of course they failed in many a way,
for the crime they brought in their day.
Religion for many just doesn't seem to be the spiritual way.

Doesn't the Age of Aquarius mean to unite?
Isn't that what religions are meant to do on this dark night,
for all the followers of these different ways
share the same fate, warming days?

The Treason of Humanity

That other path

The path of daily life is preset and often bound to a path of repetition; but human destiny may be free,
nothing and no-one knew where that would lead to be.
There are many rules which we know so little of, but 'Time' itself must enter here and be a part of anything that we seek to start.
'Time' is limited to the living, a dying Art.

Humans were given a special gift: to 'become aware' and bring attention to the moment of 'being there'.

To sense themselves in the scheme of life, the lower and the higher to be joined like two sides of the same coin, each to play its own part, then two will become one in the 'Game of Life', an Art.

All games have rules that cannot be broken, for then there'd be no game. In this way, rules are just another name for 'laws',
there is no 'just because'.

Wealth for humans allows the possibility to be free of many things; we're told with the pursuit of wealth comes the slavery it brings.
It leads us to another path, where the cause becomes the effect and the effect becomes the cause.

We lost the gift to look inside to see what goes on deep in there, we became concerned with outer things, with actions and their ways,
so that we do not look into our-self in our every-day.
Distracted we became from the aim of the game.

But we are vain in the main, so 'off-course' we think we know,
and we do not wish to leave our vanity induced show,
for that would give us such a shock, we'd be 'stumm' we couldn't talk.

Humans may give up many things, but not what their vanity brings, all the things about the self that it does love, a picture, where we see ourselves and projects unfortunately;
that is how we self-protect. We don't like our vanity to be scratched or hurt or

our pride offended or dented.
We do not like to feel we have been condescended.

So many things come close to the bone,
eat the flesh, but leave the marrow alone.

There's intelligence that's always there, it's everywhere,
it simply needs to be tapped to awaken;
with education we've been mistaken.
Indoctrination it was never meant to be, awareness from our mind was
meant to set us free, not lead us into a time of slavery,
that traps us into a circle of habitual repetition,
and draws us along the path of attrition.

This barbaric onslaught of media into the minds of our young
is a mindless education that leaves their souls stung.
It's too difficult for kids to escape from this attack on the senses of their soul,
sensitive sentient beings left un-whole.

So yes, it's a dangerous path we now tread; this leads our children down a
road of woe. Our education is a media show,
to trap them into a consumer and placid life,
where they have no intelligent choice;
we have taught them to stifle their voice.
Education: to draw water from a well,
not to stuff full off from the media we sell.

The reasoning of ordinary man is through knowledge,
but the way of a 'normal' man in touch with himself,
would be through a developed understanding of his inner health.

The 'Age of Reason', was wrongly coined, closer would have been for
humanity, the 'Age of Treason', in our time,
taken and guided down a path. So many were led and deceived
into a way of life that they thought they believed;

after all it was the 'Age of Reason',
no-one thought it could be 'Treason'.

Divided into middle and a lower class, treated like cattle 'en masse',
educated to be subdued, a process often renewed.
So now, we reach the 'Age of Conceit',
where it will get warmer as a treat.
No voice to raise, no power to be,
this was the 'Treason of Humanity'.

Doors of Deception

Leaders who don't lead, these we do not need

Something guides our leaders into believing what they think or feel to be
true, but they're obviously lost and don't know what to do.
'Selling Death' is the easy option in life,
to cultivate a world based on one of strife.

That has been the way for an aeon now, but we've reached a precipice
where that has led to somehow.
They sell death needlessly; to propagate the world at large,
and sow the seeds of misfortune and death.
Cruelty and deception comes only from a lack of real perception.

Perception of the self - what you really are and do,
unfortunately it's personal; and it's a world we often never knew.
If you're brought up to be conditioned into your role in place and time,
then often "all the world is a stage" and you play your role just fine.
Until you question yourself about what it is you do,
but unfortunately, you can live without ever being you.

You can keep that role you were assigned, but it's only the role in your mind,
selling death and deception is 'just' a lack of perception. 'Just' is such a
simple word, often spoken, never heard.

There will be a weight upon you as you try to 'sell death and deception' as
you 'lie' to a better world and 'a passion to be'.
It needs to come to your-self in silence and see,
if that's ever possible
it will disappear gradually,
or even in a moment. You will forget what you once did see
and you'll be selling death once again happily.

But a feeling may still resonate, as you decide on humanities fate.
If you're 'selling death and deception',

the 'role' you play may be in question.

Humanity does not have much time, all will not be well, nor fine.
Our leaders drive us down a one way street,
and it's a warming end that we will meet,
if the nuclear doesn't hit us in their deadly selling thirst.

The fossil fuels must stay in the ground, every little bit we've now found, step
no more through that deadly door, cease the war against the people of our
planet, stop selling death and deception.
Do what you can do, to bring yourself back to you, there's a deeper self -
inside the one you see,
when you look in the mirror of how to be, this is felt silently.

Question what it is you do, is it good for humanity or just for you?
If you played your role well, will you be proud your child to tell,
don't leave it too late, our time is running out, don't wait.

Regardless of the deception that we see,
brought to us through media and T.V.
to deceive in cultivating needs,
to trap us in a web of selling deathly seeds,
there's still something we can do.
If the sellers of deception could see through themselves -
the one they thought they knew -
that, of course, may be the hardest thing to do,
to find the 'passion to be', to be - just.

Selling death and deception, such a great misconception,
of how humanity could succeed
to help our planet in its hour of need.

Leaders without 'being', leaders who do not care,
leaders that succumb to selling death somewhere,
leaders who don't lead,
these we do not need.

Each Man *Casts a* Shadow

In days of old when Jung was bold, and he was all the rage,
he taught an idea that we should hold near,
especially relevant in our age.
It's an idea that in other forms was 'anciently' taught,
that 'each man casts a shadow',
but not the one that we see with our eye
It stems from inside and is within all,
usually, it manifests when we speak in the first form and say 'I'.
This shadow is the part of us that we do not see,
and each one casts it unconsciously.

For each and every human, this shadow is tied to their mast,
but the shadow that we should consider
is the one that humanity has cast.
As a race of beings we seem to have 'missed the mark'.
If we have an essence from the stars, all it needed was a spark.
But the shadow cast upon our being
affects us all and what we're seeing.
Jung taught that for it to change,
our inner vision must bring it within our range,
to become conscious of our shadow that is upon our being,
to become aware of something that we really are not seeing.

To light the spark that starts the flame,
the fire that burns in humanity's name, 'wise-man',
who's buried somewhere deep inside,
but the shadow's dark, so he can hide.
To cast a little light onto the darkness of this human night,
it's an individual choice, it may be weak, but you do have a voice.
And it is whispering to you, all the time,
often we do not listen, because we think we're fine.

The collective shadow cast by humans
has now led to the world we have, that heats.
To our sense of time, it may seem slow,
but to the Earth-time, it's all in a day in the evolutionary show.
The collective shadow can only be disappeared in parts,
for each individual human lightening the darkness,
must become an Art,
for no-one else will shine the light into the darkness of your night.
It's you who must make this choice,
if we wish to survive, if we wish to have a voice.

Life is hard and sometimes seems the same every day;
looked at from only one point of view, it may well be that way,
after all, your body lives and dies in time
and perceives things, ill or fine.
But your mind can perceive of finer things,
you can tune it to a higher calling,
look at time and space as if through it, you are falling.
Then the events that you encounter in your groundhog day,
you may take them in a different way,
and not react as you normally do;
you may start to sense something else
you may become aware of a 'being' called 'you'.

A being that moves through time and space,
but whose spark, whose essence is from another place;
it's been simply covered by our shadow,
of what we thought - of ourselves - it's what we bought,
paid for with attention and the ability to sense who we really are.
We call ourselves a name and stick a label on a jar,
satisfied that what we see, we will always be.

Now there are some that hear a higher calling
and through time you may not be simply falling,
you may hold the moment and sometimes be aware,
then you 'know yourself', you have a foot upon the stair.
How far do you climb? How far do you tread?

It's so easy to fall asleep and go back to your bed;
but the time is now, it always was, it never is 'just because'.

The human shadow has spread too much;
we need to bring the balance back, to equalize the scales -
otherwise all humanity fails.

So, those of you that are aware and see the shadow upon the stair: it's time.
Eternity cuts through the line of time,
just because it spirals, it won't always be fine.
There is an end part, when there is time no more – for us – then life
continues through a different door,
and that path we do not wish to take, it's humanity that's at stake.
So go down deep and rise up within,
help humanity escape this horrendous tragic fate,
fatal in the sense of final, for that is what it seems to be,
this shadow that we have cast over you, over me.

There will be no more higher calling now,
unless humanity's helped somehow.
Sense yourself as you read these words,
feel and think about what you read, do you think you can succeed?
Or is it back to sleep and back to bed,
drop the veil again over the head,
on with the day, in any old, same old, same old way.

So many things to occupy your mind, so many thoughts fly on by,
some you'll go with, some you won't,
some you want, some you don't.
Grab an eagle if you can, it soars high above the human man,
sees things from a higher place - only humans in a race -
racing through time, thinking all will be fine,
injected with the disease of to-morrow.
Things may get better in time and ease our sorrow,
tomorrow we'll be fine.
Unfortunately, that was part of the trick;
humans occupied themselves with anything and everything
and became a little sick.

They fell out of balance with themselves,
affected their future and their planet's health.
A race of 'beings' sent down to wonder, become aware and to care for one
thing and all.

The essence of each travelled from the stars;
it was a long trip. They got lost and abandoned their ship
and the balance they did tip.
In part for most, a 'being' unaware,
except for petty concerns about which they did care,
inane trivialities that kept them from seeing that there was a stair,
to lead them back to where they belong;
but for that they need to hear and sing a different song,
one in which they have a voice, for they really do have a choice.

But if you don't hear it, back to bed, go to sleep,
with inane trivia, stuck in your head.
But if, as Mr Thoreau said, you hear a different tune,
and a different calling, then, when you request, it will respond,
and through time you may not be falling,
you will hold that moment called 'Now';
and perhaps you will help chase that shadow from the wall somehow, to
help yourself and all humankind,
to be free of the chains that hold us, face down and keep us blind.

Then one day, maybe, who knows,
perhaps we can bring the scales back on track,
to stop humanity from this unconscious self-attack, to bring us back to what
should be near, this way was never meant to be,
but what do you think, feel or see?

Tame the Dragon

Tame the Dragon, it's a beast;
in mythical and allegoric it has much that is symbolic,
but now, these days, nature is its feast.
The Dragon of the human race, the personality, it's been displaced.
We're working from a place that isn't real;
at least it doesn't correspond to how we feel.

Tame the Dragon, it's a beast, that doesn't mean to stop its feast,
it means there are some things we should reform,
before this monstrosity becomes the norm -
if we're not too late already.
We have to find a balance and a hope that would keep us steady,
to hold our course as nature changes path,
Global Warming has an aftermath.

Tame the Dragon, it's a beast,
and there's much that we should cease.
Burning poisonous energy fuels from the ground,
should be the first call in helping to cease this monstrous sound,
but it's a many headed beast,
the 'War on 'Earth' machine that doesn't cease.

Tame the Dragon, it is a beast,
tame the fire, control its head, there's no way it will be dead.
Many ancient pictures of symbolic imagery
show that the Dragon should be controlled, not slayed;
the spear is held above the mouth or head;
the threat is there to be read.

Tame the Dragon, it's a beast,
as a collective human race, our Dragon's reached a mighty pace.
The society of the selfish we are being educated to be,
it goes on almost undetected, almost invisibly.
Our voice is silent, our will to be is trashed and trodden,
that Dragon – we are – seems to be forgotten.

The sensual mind, the man of the senses, this he may not see,
for the Dragon works invisibly.
So sometimes it's hard to believe if these things you can't perceive.
If you cannot see and feel and touch,
then you never know when it's too much,
for that, often we must be taught;
but perception isn't something that can be bought.

It's perception of all you need to be informed, then alarmed,
then perhaps your attention will not be farmed
by those who seek to 'occupy' your mind and leave you like the three wise
monkeys, deaf, dumb and blind.
Waking to the horror of the Dragon at the wheel,
it's driving us down the path and it's a Global Warming that we feel. So tame
the Dragon, it's a beast and upon all humanity it does feast.

Angels and Animals

Something above and something below, we seem to be stuck in the middle,
sometimes this is something we know.

It's formulated in many different ways, but the action's the same in
everybody's days: our attention is taken and we become immersed –
identified in ourselves, a role that seems well rehearsed.

The play of life unfolds before our very eyes but without awareness there's
no understanding of the events of the surprise.
The angel in us is waiting for the animal to abate,
and the animal is in denial,
the angel turns its back with a sad smile,
for it's delicate and cannot be forced.

There is a need to find a common direction,
that's hard to find without detection,
for it needs humans to become aware, a quality that's often not there, lost in
the animal world of senses and concern, taken by the trivia that we presume
gives meaning to our life.

There is a spark within, waiting to burn, waiting to become a flame; but one
has to separate from oneself – from even one's own name, in order to find
this common aim.

Man is undoubtedly stuck 'between the devil and the deep blue sea'
and it's been said that that is his destiny,
or his spirit was sown 'between a rock and a hard place',
a divine spark, stuck with a human face.

To confront our lower nature has been a long evolutionary race,
one that we seem to be losing at an increasing pace,
the lower rejects, does the higher suspect – that there is no hope.

Unfortunately, time itself becomes a problem now,
our planet warms – and conditions will change for most of life forms.

For the Earth it's no big deal, it's just a moment in the universal zeal.

As the pendulum swings from one extreme to another,
Earth in its own time will recover.
Many ancient stories tell of how the pendulum swings,
in everything there is an opposite in what it brings.
Inside man and the outside world,
it seems there are connected strings always being unfurled.
The pendulum swings from one side to the other,
love begets hate or hate begets love,
it seems one only has to wait for the other.

From civilization to barbarism that seems to be our waiting fate.
It would take a movement of the human race
to hold Global Warming down a pace.
There is much that distracts us all;
but there is only one generation left before this fall,
and it will be our falling and our fault
if Global Warming we cannot halt.

'Nothing Too Much' (II)

"The ancient Delphic temples had a saying about inner wealth
'Know thy-self', it's said so much it's lost its meaning -
rarely said with real feeling.

There was another, mostly forgotten now, but it was there anyhow,
as equal to the other.
It was placed to bring a balance to the human race,
'Nothing too much'."

Two instructions for their path, 'know thyself',
what you are - what you do and its aftermath.
'Nothing too much' was to bring a balance - come back to a centre, for they
said there was always a law that always did enter,
like all actions in life, a pendulum did swing
between one extreme and another for everything.
It's talked about in many ways, simplified by some in what they say.

There is a time for action and a time for rest, there is a time for joy and a
time for sorrow, if not today it may be tomorrow.
A time of war, a time of peace, a time of plenty, a time of famine, the list is
endless, it seems there's nothing to be done, except for one thing,
to take the power of the extremes out from under them.

This of course was meant to be an inward task,
to take the power away from the mask
that we all wear, almost all the time,
even when we're alone, we're almost never fine.
Something nags inside and burns, embers in the dark,
like Cinderella waiting for that spark
to rise from the ashes of our daily life,
to deal with life differently, for it's mostly strife,
to bring a balance back to oneself,
to find 'the pearl', they say of 'inner wealth'.

Well, easier said than done,
not much time for that
if you have to find food for your daughter or your son.
But none the less, for some, that possibility is always there, just taking a
step a little higher up that stair.

'Nothing too much' was the second idea,
but know thyself was the first to appear,
you need to know to what extremes you draw near,
in order to take the power away from those extremes every day.
How to take the power and force away from resentment, anger, fear,
jealousy, meanness, laziness, judging, conceit, the list of course goes on
and on, they all have their opposites in some strange ways, these things
affect us all our days.
Something we all can recognize of where we are,
and where that power lies.

For that's the law it seems to be, that we can only be aware of one side of
the swing of the pendulum, we see.
That may be why they say people are blind
for that second law we cannot find,
or at least, not remember or be not aware that there's a swing happening
everywhere.

For our planet, unfortunately, we are on an extreme side: the tendency is to
getting warm, so that every day is the norm.
There was a time to take oil and gas out the ground,
obviously those are what we found,
but western man with his civilized ways, has left the world in a daze.
And it continues up till now, for major companies don't know how to stop
themselves. We have gone over to an extreme.
Burning oil, it's not a dream, it's a nightmare, and as there's no sound in
space, they'll be no-one to hear us scream.

Everything we do today now takes us away – there's no way to 'know
thyself', for what is it that you know? That part of you that loves the trivia
show, that's fascinated with the candyfloss of life, okay, its manipulated now
today, but it's always been that way.

'Humans, let's confuse them and occupy them so they have no say,
we'll steal their awareness and energy and we'll do it every day.
There's a multitude of activities and emotions that will occupy their whole life. We'll activate their thought process a little so they think they know the meaning of what it is they're feeling;
but we'll keep them only self-aware, it will keep them out of balance with themselves, even if they dare.
They'll think that that shadow on the wall is really a picture of their health we will occupy them so that if they recognize their state and want to break free they'll have to suffer and pay a very high fee.

But now, time for them is no longer their friend, so many humans lost their way, only a few come back every day,
not enough to make a change, humans have moved out of range.
They lost their balance and a contact with something that is real;
they substituted it for the trivia deal.
And in worshiping themselves and what little insight and worldly power they had, they lost their planet, yes, it's sad.
But life goes on until it stops, and "the real never ceases to be".
Sadly it's only the unreal that they see,
so for them, yes, life goes on until it stops.
They lost their balance, they lost their way,
'humans', have nothing too much to say.'

Sense of Humour

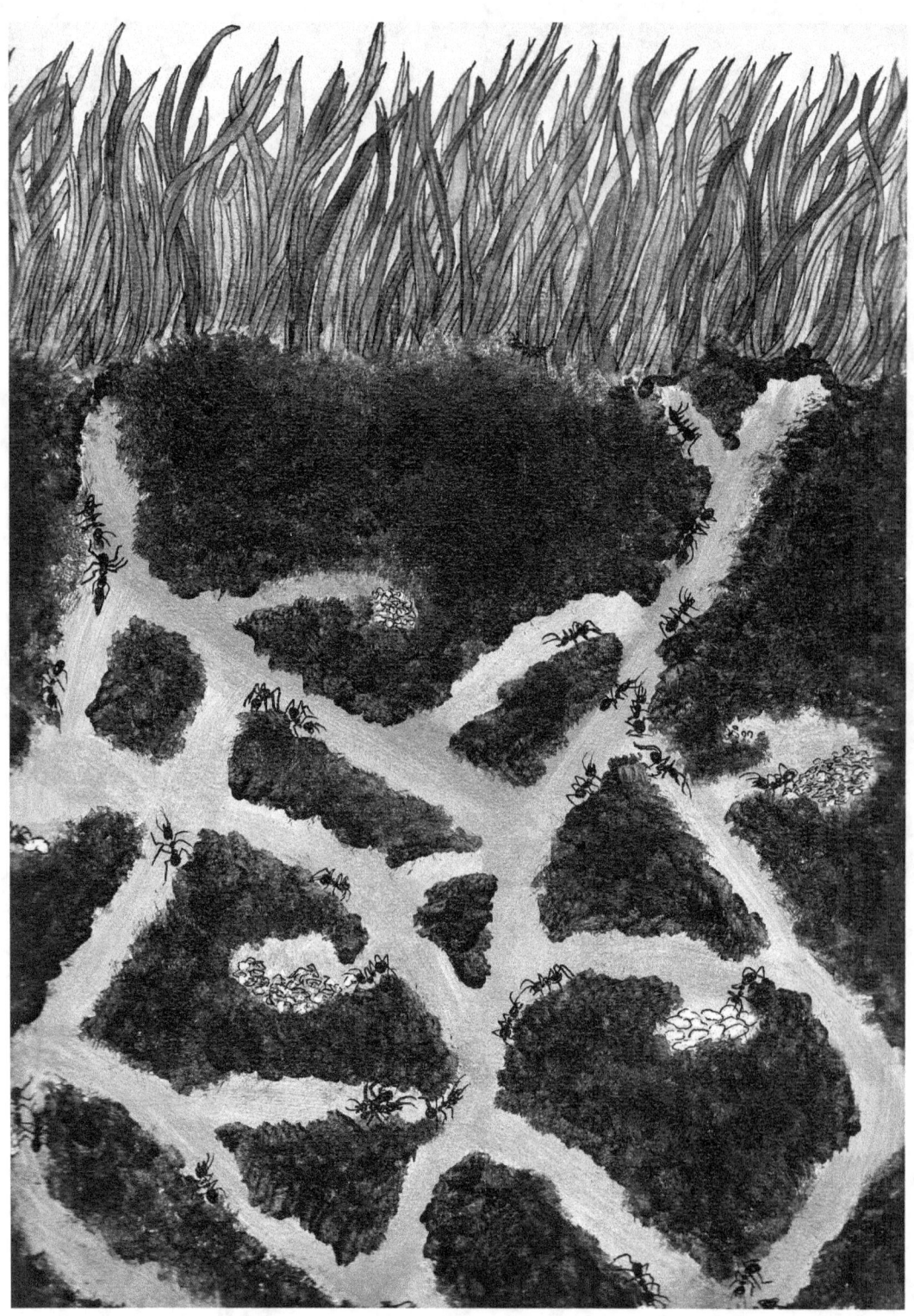

Ants and the stories they tell

'Have you heard the latest news?'

'No, what?'

'We're going to be made big again; humans have screwed up; so we get a second chance.'

'Oh, that's great; will we get Atomics this time?'

'We don't need Atomics; we can carry more than ten times our body weight, defend with poison, and have powerful pincers and teeth. We can communicate with these dangly things on top of our head, we have built in air conditioning in underground housing. Global warming will not affect us, and when we're bigger we will have no predators. We'll be the top predator on the planet again. And there are billions of us.'

'Will we still have to have perpetual wars and takes slaves?'

'I think so, why not?

'It's just that I'm sure that was a reason we were made small in the first place.'

'Oh, I heard about that, I think it was because we managed to create a totalitarian state, where everyone was working for the sake of the home-hill.'

'But isn't that, what humans are doing now?'

'Yes, of course, but their intelligence isn't very good, they destroy their surroundings and make life unbearable for everything else on the planet: their very ways of existence destroy the habitat, so they're stupid really; no other living thing does that.

We were made small because we lost our chance at individuality, humans have lost theirs now as well, but we are more helpful for the planet, as it slowly changes. Many of the bigger things will die out in the heat. Yup, and we're the most organized and smartest of all beings that can live underground, so we get a second chance to rule the roost.'

'What's a roost?'

'It's where chickens live.'

'What are chickens?'

'Big fat birds, that can't fly.'

'Well if they can't fly, why are they called birds?'

'They have wings.'

'Well, why can't they fly then?'

'They're too fat to fly, humans breed them on theirs farms, like we use our slaves in our farms, some for work, others for food.'

'Humans seem a lot like us really, don't they?'

'No, they're ugly monsters, giant beasts, but we were their size once, and we will be again it seems. Our underground work will reorganize the planet again, over time it will recover and we will be left in charge.'

'Can we keep chickens?'

Little Bear

I'm a little bear who likes honey, and I don't I know what to do.
It's getting a little hot and I'm worried about me and you,
you see I also like to climb trees,
but I heard the other day that global warming's under way
and if there are no trees there will be no birds and no bees,
and there'd be no honey! Really, is there nothing you can do?

Don't you like trees and honey too?
I really don't know what to do and I'm worried through and through.
I sleep in a tree, my, oh my, what will become of me.
Trees are nice and warm and strong,
they should stay where they belong,
I sleep in a hollow tree and there are a lot of bears who are small like me,
we really need a tree, but honey too would be a treat.
Please save the trees.

I wrote a song just for you, so you can sing my song and share it too:

'Save the bees, save the bees, and the trees,
don't you know we really need these?
Don't burn the oil, please don't burn the oil,
walk around like me; you too can climb a tree.'

Dear Santa,

You're going to lose your job, no more snow at Christmas time,
but don't worry; you'll be fine.

Your home is melting, you'd better move.
I think the reindeers would approve.
Your house will start to melt and it will drop all around,
and pretty soon there'll be no more ice or snow to be found.
Where you live will become deep water blue,
I'm afraid that there's nothing you can do.

We, the people, that you give the Christmas spirit to
have heated the world, it will burn through.
So for Christmas time for a few years,
please give us presents to sooth our fears.
I hope you manage it again one day to find it in your heart to say,
Merry Christmas.
Ps. if you're not too busy, could I have all my presents now please?

Will we miss it - Society - Life?

The Sadness of Society

Dear Grandchildren, I thought I'd write and say a few words about the good and bad things of what you are probably going through by now, or that still may be to come in your globally warming world.

You will find in the following list it's not all bad, there's always a little good and bad to everything, although you may have to look for it, this is true. But it's a little tongue in cheek, which is not meant to be negative, it's just a little fun to lighten the inherent load of such a heavy topic. Life is not only about surviving the heat and finding food and water, well, okay, for you, by now it will be, but...

I can only imagine your living conditions, it's predicted that at some point in the not too distant future civilization will collapse and therefore society can no longer run, millions of people all stuck together and fighting over what they can get. I envision this with great sadness.

In our times the powerful controllers tried to tell us that Global Warming wasn't real, that it wasn't happening. They spent a lot of money and effort on trying to keep people in the dark about what was befalling our world, instead of doing something about it.

Oh, by the way, in case you're wondering about that word 'money'. Money was just a common coin that we exchanged between each other when we wanted to have something like food or clothing etc. It was okay for a while but it changed into a strange system where most of the money only went to a few people in charge and the rest of the people which is about 99% of the world's population had to struggle for the aforementioned goods.

Due to certain strange abnormalities contained within that system called capitalism, they caused our world to heat. You will know all about that by now of course.

'They, our leaders', tried to stop us from preventing our world, now yours, from heating. All of this you will be experiencing. These few words were just to connect it up for you as we don't really know how information will be given to you or exchanged in your times.

You will probably miss the sensation of a cool breeze on a hot summer day; unfortunately, every day will be summer for you. In your time it's predicted to be too hot to be outdoors in the hot hours, which will be most of the time: due to the amount of carbon trapping the heat all around the planet.

According to our people of science, humans seemed to have appeared on the planet when conditions and temperature were just right for our existence, strange that, isn't it? But then we speed heated the planet due to overuse of fossil fuels that lead to the destruction of the eco systems that we have. We left no barriers that helped to neutralize the effects of what we did. We went over the tipping point. And we are sorry, well, most of us at least.

Some people say or believe that we're just one little experiment of many in the vast operational machinery of organic life on Earth, and that organic life is like a big transformer of energies. It receives energies and transforms them; so it seems, we failed to recognize our purpose. We are different than other beings, even other humanoid branches that existed before us; we had the possibility of becoming self-conscious, self-aware. Not just of living and reacting, but of contemplating – a being aware – cognitive thinking, planning, conceptualizing, empathizing and wishing.

It seems, school is out and we don't get to sit the test again. We'll just give you here a few comments on the dark gallows side, for what you are probably living through now could be summed up in three words: Hell on Earth.

You will have no more coffee - mornings will be hell.

No more T.V. - Whao, no more embedded thoughts. Suggestions, able to live in the present moment of reality – that will be Hell.

No more changing of the seasons – saves money on clothing.

No more worries about being over-weight – food will be scarce, but it's easier to find clothing.

No more thinking 'life is a game' - in your face survival will be the order of the day.

No more having to make those top ten wish lists of things you always wanted to do - life will be limited.

No more waiting on busses - there won't be any.

No more queues in shops - there won't be any.

No more having to go on the internet - as above.

No more of choosing subjects in school - survival classes will be the main subject in home education.

No need to worry about eating too much sugar - non-available.

No need to worry about paying for health care - no social structure to have any.

No need to worry about whether it will rain today or not - in many parts of the world - it won't.

No need to worry about the weather at all - every day will be mostly the same.

No need to worry about food for the dog or cat - you'll be eating them by now.

No need to worry about different religions and which one is right for you. But then again religion may have turned into something even weirder than it is today.

No need to worry about old age pension and survival - there might not be any old and you might not make it.

No more the trouble of going through shops looking for new stuff to buy and all the thousands of choices of everything available - you wouldn't want that any longer, would you?

You won't become addicted to coffee or cigarettes, which is a blessing for you believe me. Every day having to make coffee and inhale nicotine into your body and make companies rich by killing yourself slowly, it's a drag really; you're much better off without them.

You will have no more sitting in cars and making long-distance travel that was dangerous, traveling at such high speeds with no real protection, accidents happened all the time; more people died from that than in wars.

A problem also that you won't know about in your days is that you won't have to worry about dying from a heart attack from eating all of the chemicals in foods that we have in our days. The multiple choices of poisons were killing us. Once again, that also killed more people than wars. Really, we used poisons that made food look better to eat but was bad for us, rather than food that had no poisons and didn't look so good. Strange, don't you think?

If you are able enough to read these words, then you're still doing okay, as they say. But for your kids and theirs, as you will know by now, education is on its way out.

You also may not have what we call electricity. In our darkened rooms we have that form of energy for artificial light, powered by cables of wire that ran through our cities. If you are wondering what that was like by now, well, just look up at your wonderful 'Sky Art' that no doubt you have very regularly now, lightning, in many places where you still have rain. The combination of no rain or water on some parts of the planet and way too much in other places must be interesting and devastating for you.

On the extreme heavy side of life: many people will have to move, millions; and they won't be going back home again. Due to the changes that you will be going through, there will be wars of resources, water, food, land. The poor of the world and the hardest hit will be trying to reach places of safety out of dire need to save their children. Many will die on the way and the governments or companies that will take care of border control by your time may simply kill the excessive population.

Many justifiable reasons will be given, your own safety, your own needed resources and you may well agree and this will be the sadness of society.

Please excuse my ending on a sombre note, but I can only imagine your horror, and it may well be worse than what I imagine. Perhaps between now and your time, things will have changed possibly for the better or at least not be so dramatically bad. That, I'm afraid is unlikely. Unless the age of now, turns into an 'Age of Change', all social life towards more humanitarian ways, it will lead to the 'Age of Barbarism' before the planet heats too much for life itself to exist.

Which, if you're not there already, it's where you will be heading. If so, my deepest regrets. It means the people of my age, now, were not able to rise to the call to become Heroes for you, myself included. So now, all I will leave you with are a few words from ancient times.

Born alive, born to die?
No. The real never ceases to be.
The real lives inside you and I.
A body it inhabits for but a moment of time.
Something that's real can never cease to be.

Dear GOD

Dear God,

We lost our balance; help us bring it back. Be careful, we're under attack. They have power and guns. Surveillance means nowhere to run. Why did you let them do it? Perhaps you never knew it; perhaps you set the rules of the game of life in place. Perhaps you had no need to look back at the human race. Could it be true, that life is just a race; against time, will we ever look upon your face? A burning bush, a thunderous voice, anything really would do. We don't really have a choice. We try to look inside, but we've been manipulated, so we watch T.V. and enjoy the ride. We're given many distractions, but we still recognize our 'being-less' leader's actions. What can we do? Is it up to us or you?

A small detail in passing: I've only recently heard the news. It was said in our ancient times that a life-time of a human being was but the twinkling of an eye for you, in other words about 80 years (an average lifetime) down here on our heating planet, is for you, like an eye blink. We have a saying, 'blink and you miss it', well, just in case you blinked and missed the last hundred years or so, let's bring you up to date.

The 'social' system most of the world is under these days is often called 'Predatory Capitalism'. Understanding the depth and implications of the first word, should give you the idea, which is intrinsically linked financially with the mis-use of the natural resources on your planet and sadly its warming destruction due to anthropogenic over-use of fossil fuels. (I just know you'll understand that.)

As you probably know and understand in your instant appreciation of everything: we're burning all the oil and other stuff causing a heating and poisoning of your planet. Of course some of us are sorry and of course some don't care. In our modern expression, which if you did blink, will certainly bring you up to date on our attitude problem, "shit happens".

Wars of destruction, bringing a mass of death and devastation to all, are fought for maintaining this system of access and control of these planetary resources. Our natural empathies are deliberately diverted into trivia or survival, and often not developed enough to care beyond our nearest and dearest.

We have a planet with 2 billion of its population who go to sleep every night starving, and untold millions under the action of occupation and the business of war. The starving, the suffering, the exploited and dying are marginalized to the outer rim of our awareness. The poor are in their billions.

This is the reality of the situation. Less than a mere 1% of the population amass and control financial wealth; enough people to fit on one of our modern, but probably for you out of date, double decker buses, while the majority, the other 99% of the world's people simply suffer in various ways until they die. Not nice, is it? Now this probably wasn't what you had planned, because if you planned it, well then, you only have yourself to blame, so let's give you the benefit of the doubt.

Sorry to inform you, but in case you had a long eye blink moment, as we all do sometimes, you know the saying, 'as above so below'. We just thought we'd fill you in on the last eye blink. Any helpful non-devastation 'End of World' solutions to help bring a balance back would be most appreciated.

Yours sincerely

Your Children

Ps, just as a personal comment: It's a helluva way to treat your family.

Is Beelzebub Sad?

Is it possible Beelzebub is sad, and doesn't know what to do,
this Planet 'being' his home too?

He losses something to a climatic finale of lust and greed, it must have
seemed it was all he'd ever need. But all 'Good' things must come to pass,
the 'humans' seem to have died of greed, greed for the unnatural way of life;
it fed so much worldly strife.

Supposedly, he was here for humans to test, to work against him and try to
do their best, to find the better side of themselves alive, to be 'quickened' to
the core,
to keep apace and keep abreast, and 'be themselves' once more.

Beelzebub didn't come to watch a Planet go up in flames.
People say it's his home, but he doesn't hold 'the reigns'.
If he could change it I suppose he would, for although he was fallen, his
name was 'Light-Bearer' in a world of darkness.

He was a favourite of the Heavenly 'Good',
if all things were meant to be, then Beelzebub's fall he did foresee.
A war in Heaven, a war in Hell,
it seems that there's always a war of which we can tell.

Of course, humans see with only human perception,
that itself may lead to much deception.
For the 'mysteries' and science now, tell us it's a fact,
that for much of what we see and perceive we're slightly off the track, and a
man, as much as he thinks he's vertical,
simply finds it hard to get off his back,
asleep to senses that lie unseen, deep within the darkest dream.

Some say Beelzebub is a being of strange and clever wit, he'd make a deal
for the fun of it; that's if you listen to the Christian view of life. But the
concept of good and evil did appear,
along with the Zoroastrians, who held it rather dear.

Of all these things there's obviously much one can say,
but remember, who it is that writes and controls 'history'.

Control the record; control the past,
then many things can be 'trashed'.
From the translators or the scribes, many have altered very much, due to
ignorance or bribes.
So how can we truly tell if the words we read are truly well
and in accord with the fact?

As time tells the history only of crime,
we never know what 'truth' we find.
In generations through the ages
the deviations came with the pages.

Two histories always run through time, one is coarse - one is fine.
The history that may affect us all
could have been the one of the higher call.

Yes, the Devil is probably sad indeed,
for with no people he will be in need.
Perhaps he will return himself to his father,
his original wealth and become the 'bearer of light' once more,
if he bends his knee and knocks upon the door.
Who can tell the history of things that we cannot truly see;
what was once is not always how it has to be.

SENSELESS WAR

Common War

War is not an exception – it has always been so. Therefore it seems difficult anywhere else to go. But we are humans in a race and the race is against time. And we've come to a problem that we've never had to face – Global Warming.

Everything holds us back from struggling against this merciless attack. Laws and regulations, organized austerity upon the nations by those who rule from above; there is no common human love, only a desire for profit to make those chains are tight and hard to break.

War is simply another tool, but it's an event that is inhumanly cruel. In general, our societies have developed to recognize this truth: people don't want to send their kids off to die, for there is no real reason why. These days now it's just another manipulated event, manipulate the people, play with their mind – organize their emotions on anything to vent; it's only the 99% that go off to war, they are the blind.

Our planet has become so civilized that we destroy countries that don't want to be privatized. Strange entities have been given power over the common people all over our world. It's now legal in our laws that they're entitled to sharpen their claws and 'they' are the beast of prey. And a beast of prey will not let you go, not once it holds you down below. "Power concedes nothing without a demand", so what must we demand for this beast of prey to understand, that we need a planet to live, that we need a planet to our children give.

At this stage in human history and the unfolding of our mystery, human time runs out. This is a calculated attack from this beast of prey on our back. We need to shake the beast off and cause him to back off, to release the common people from the bonds of oppression and fear, to allow a new humanity to appear. There's a generation left of chance, it's not romance. One voice, one cause, Global Warming laws, but for that to succeed, social laws we need. Common heroes we need in every land – imminent human extinction we must now understand. We're on a speeding train and we have no break, the beast of prey we must shake.

1% WAR:

"Yes, of course we send your kids off to war and yes, it's true, you don't really know what you're fighting for. If you did you wouldn't go, it's as simple as that, you wouldn't join our show and a show it is most of the time. We need your boys to stand in line – to die.

Our psychologists supply us the information and show us the way, where we may enter your mind and do so all the time. Propaganda got such a bad name that we had to reinvent ourselves; so public relations became the game. It's one of the biggest businesses in all lands; it's something that you will never truly understand.

Embedded thoughts make you think anything we desire, it turns you into a puppet on a string: the working class, stuck in the mire. We let you breed, we have a need that your kids go off to war and die. We fixed it in your education; we blasted your mind without cessation with thoughts that hold you fixed to the dream and this is   how it's always been.

It's big business for us that you go off to kill and die. War must be a horror, we don't send our own kids off to war; we're rich and we really know what we're fighting for. We need to sow destruction and terror through all other lands; there's a Global Warming coming; one day this you will understand.

Even if there wasn't we'd still start wars; business is still the same, it makes no difference to our aims. They say money makes the world go round, well, it doesn't really, but none the less we try to get as much as can be found.

War is just another measure that we inflicted on you. We left you unemployed and uneducated, so, you've got nothing better to do. The newer generations we occupy with toys of war, fire bullets on a screen, it makes a flash; war seems fun and clean. They get so good they think they can go off and fight for real; you don't realize that your soul we steal.

We confuse you in so many ways and we do it till the end of your days. Some of you of course do suspect and you taste the lie that you detect; but we keep at it all the time, we bombard every thought in your mind. We turn you into the savage state; we turn you into the lowest form of man; we do all this because we can. We turn your boys into killing monsters at the end; they think they're dying for their friends; we embed the buddy, buddy thing; it brings us money, that song you sing."

The 1% are always at war with the 99% of the human race, as well as everything else on this planet. When you seek to dominate and control everything, whether psychological or physical then you are always at war, at war in yourself, never at peace.

WAR

Class War

It's personal and it's not personal, it's the system. It's made that way, its rules are 'the people slay'. It's personal and it's class war, it's personal we're fighting and we know what for.

Your troubles are personal and you don't know what to do; it's a class war and they're pissing on you. So yea, it's gonna rain and it's gonna rain pain. The poor stay poor while the rich only gain, a class war it's always been. It's a system that's overseen by those who want to regulate and control humankind as a whole.

There is always a war of which we can speak; it's the war of the rich and powerful on the weak. The weak and the poor of the human race, we are so many it's a nameless face. By comparison 'they' are few, Our future 'they' have shod, for it seems 'they' worship strange Gods, the Gods of love of power, love of the rich, love of the self, 'they' scratch their itch. 'They' only look to the god of wealth. That's where 'they' live and move and have their being, 'they' do this with their eyes open wide, but there's something they're not seeing.

Humankind itself will fade from this place, and it won't be a fading, it will be as if in a race. The predicted heat brings different effects of devastations, and all combined, nature loses its creations. So this war against the 99% of humanity comes from an attitude that's actually insanity. We've let the insane take over and rule our planet. Damn it.

Children Sent To War

Children, sent to war, often don't know what they're fighting for.
Filled with media propaganda since childhood;
they grow up thinking war is good.
It's embedded in our neuron network,
firing off the sparks of excitement and expectation,
until faced with a reality,
that maybe killing people isn't just how life should be.

It's mostly the young sent off to die; if they return, suicide is high.
On average it's one boy every hour who takes his own life,
once they've returned from a war of strife.
Who are you fighting for and who are you dying for?
There are many reasons for kids to go to war to kill.
It's often embedded in the media thrill.
The hormones kick in, the neurons fire;
it gets meshed up in the emotional wire.

There are also economic reasons,
when a country keeps its young poor and unemployed
and the government offers a life which they promise will be enjoyed.
They'll teach you a trade that you may apply,
if you get lucky, if you don't die.
If the educational system is ripped apart
then 'joining up' may help you start
your way up the ladder to a wife, a family, a life.

Each man loves his own country; no man betrays it really;
no man is a traitor to the land he was born into.
It's where his ancestral blood runs through,
but it's the governing policy of those elected;
their secret financing and laws are almost undetected,
enough to confuse and befuddle a public
that they elected - to look after them.

When boys go to war they don't know what they're fighting for.
We pile their head with media noise, but all in all it's mostly boys,
teaching them to kill and not to care,

over-riding the natural instinct to love and share
their deepest sense of humanity
for something they neither understand nor see.

It's an ancient 'Art' - death and destruction,
something from which humanity will probably never part.
Regardless of how far we've come,
to 'Public Relations' we all succumb.
When boys go to war they don't know what they're fighting for.
To send a boy into war to make him a man,
is something we can never really understand.

There is no logic in that thought, and there is no heart;
from humanity we depart, when we send boys into war.
They've been pre-set from T.V. where psychologists are paid to see
how to get the emotional hooks in and drive them deep.
It begins with toys for boys, a consumer plot;
we were sold but they were bought.

The Goddess PR buys their soul; they will never now be humanly whole.
We've turned a child into a killing man,
and it's no dream that he's now a killing machine.

Embedded interests lie at heart and from humanity we did depart,
when our boys go to war. PR rules and says it's so,
but mostly these boys don't know where to go.
Knife with blood, bullet in brain, kill the mind or body, it's all pain.
Train to follow orders and do the master's will,
but it's an emotional boy who pays the bill.

Even just those who at a computer sit and press a button called 'hit',
they go home and they've been droned.
Something leaves the soul alone;
when we send our boys to war.
They've been told what they are fighting for,
to defend their land and soil;
but in reality it's often someone else's oil.

Access to resources from afar, our companies like to fill their jar. Paid with
blood, swapped for crude, things are now out of balance.

In the world today, there is no just war;

it's only what the Goddess PR does say.
Her voice is strong and well financed;
she pulls the strings and our boys dance,
not knowing that they've been pre-set,
to kill on order, as they're in the 'Net'.

There's no way we can foresee for how humanity it will be,
when we continue to send our boys to war,
and con them into thinking that they knew what they were fighting for.

People in power enjoy playing the trick.
They survive and get rich in subduing us with a carrot and stick.
All they say is 'Ain't life a bitch', for we are the class of the rich.
Our boys don't go to war, because we know what we're fighting for;
we only send the poor 'en masse', it's just the working class.

The Killing Curse

Our planet rages in WAR,
bullets and bombs drop everywhere,
ripping poor people to their blood and bone.
WAR leaves no-one alone.

Shock and awe visiting every land;
what is it of this we're meant to understand?
The killing curse upon all peoples fighting for what,
some oil and things buried in the land?

Others to defend themselves and what they understand,
mostly women, children and the old, the poor they have been told,
this is how it has to be, but not with pen or ink or even T.V.,
but with bomb and bullets killing everything they see.
Imagine the horror of that it's not possible unless there you be.

What is this that people live, fight and die for? What reason is good enough
to enter other lands to pull a trigger and blast away a family? What is it in our
education today that makes it seem that's okay?

How to stop a WAR?
Stop sending soldiers off to kill and die.
They don't know what they're dying for.
They're boys, not yet men and it's always the young and poor of every land
that are told, conditioned to join up to the killing band.
Taught that it's okay to kill, to travel over to other lands,
'Killing will make you a man'.
Well, if that were true,
then the young who survive wouldn't come back home and kill themselves,
which is what they do.

Suicide is the main cause of death of all returning home soldiers in the land.
There's something in war that they came to understand,
that it's wrong. Their leaders lied about their cause,
to make boys go against human laws.

205

Senseless War

It's a common thing to make the young (public) believe anything.
Anything at all will do, as long as they go off to kill for you.
And if they come home to kill and maim their family before their own life they
take, well, that's what's at stake.
They are many, the poor, the not working class;
that's why we have them bred 'en masse'.

We keep them indoctrinated and unemployed
and manipulate the media as if war can be enjoyed.
There's no blood to see upon a screen, these days just a flash of colour,
death is quick, there is no pain,
and if you lose, you can click again, join the game,
lots of cool guns and ways to kill, T.V. war such a thrill.
You can sit for hours and watch them play,
or join in and T.V. kill yourself every day.
And in the end the neurons in your mind are altered and changed, the
connecting paths are interlinked; now, this is how you think.

Sure, it's in the background that real people will die,
but when it's now real war you realize something was a lie.
The game is set but sadly the mind is too;
this has now become a part of you.
Repeated patterns in the brain don't reveal that you cause pain.
The blood is not upon your hand, until you're in that real battle land,
putting a real bullet through a real person's head,
and looking at the colour of real blood,
when a real person is really dead.

Eventually, if you survive and come on home and cannot deal with the inner
pain, if you don't kill others just the same,
then it's yourself you will blame, and you will die the suicide death, for you
will have come to understand, that war is not a game.

It's a whole business, how to induce boys to go to war, to numb the effects;
it's very subtle, but sometimes not.
In the last 20 years or so, it's crept into films and T.V.
Not even slowly.

They dropped the barriers down; so more violence could our society accept,
our new and young generation did not detect,
that their minds were being conditioned to change, and this accept.

Senseless War

The young of now think it was always this way,
and if they watch a film of old, to them it has nothing to say.
We put it down to 'they live in faster times',
true, but not the whole truth.

Science and behavioural conditioning came into play,
with lots of tricks to give children no say
with what penetrates into their mind. Add in education that doesn't teach
kids to think, give them games to play where they don't blink,
eyes wide, fingers at the ready; hold that moment, keep it steady
and fire the endless bullets away,
collect some points, get more every day.
It will occupy you, it's designed that way.

We can thank our behavioural scientists for that mind numbing pleasure
today, teams of psychologists working out how to get emotional hooks in
kids, when young,
so they sing the song they want sung.
To join into the consumer plot, to buy stuff that they now think that they
need, it keeps them occupied, it's a constant feed.

Humans conditioned to perform like monkeys in a cage,
having the illusion of freedom and killing is a good rage.
It's tied into the network system of the mind;
so many millions firing blind,
until old enough to go off and die for real,
for something that they've been taught to feel.
But even these days that step has been advanced.
Sit in a room and bomb from afar, and the blood and destruction and death
will never get to the screen.
You never hear where you have been,
to visit someone in another land.
Hit a button blow, them apart,
collateral damage, it's war, they understand.

It's how we are trained and conditioned to be,
the pain of others we don't see.
Our nerves are wired and it's a buzz;
and this we must do, for our society has left no other jobs for you.
Fast food and packaging is just not the same
as playing this killing game.

Senseless War

If I don't do this I'll be unemployed,
it's just as well, it's conditioned for it to be enjoyed.

Slowly as the planet heats,
I'll pass these skills onto my son, so he can have these treats.
It will become more interactive, but only to make it more attractive,
to the young minds that are waiting to be conditioned to think that war is
okay. We have to fight for space and resources on a planet that heats more
every day,
so we must kill others in distant lands far away.

Over the years it will come back home,
because as the population dies off,
there will be no power or need to roam.
To kill, it will be embedded in the brain,
as the savage state begins to reign.
It's the path to barbarism at the end.
As civilization collapses, no-one will have a friend.

What do you think people will feed on
when there's nothing to be had at the end?

Computer Karma

People stand in line for food, this is life and it isn't good
unless you're rich and can look down from above;
then it's all you see of human love.
Stand in line to buy rice or bread, our children die, left unfed.

The rich look down upon our class;
they treat us as if we are the 'untouchable' mass.
For an 'eon' now, the normal people of life you see,
struggle to survive, that's you, that's me.
We fight and die for the rich; if the roles could be reversed,
would we switch?

We are the descendants of those who
fought for the rights and the normal things to live:
the right for clean water and some food for my son or daughter,
the right to live a life of peace, the right to protest the unjust;
these rights are a must.

Powerful interests control this ship,
informed managers earn their tips;
so they retire to their house of non-being, it's got many floors and all eyes
sensing, guided complete from head to tail,
it's the unseen many-headed monster that will prevail.
It lashes out at all it sees,
its 'Net' is large and it's lost in its own make-believes.

There's no muzzle on this beast and it's delirious in its frenzied attack, out of
control, nashing and thrashing in its endeavour.
It has dug deep into the soul of man
and escape this beast, it seems, he never can.

How can you free your-self from a society of control
that refuses to recognize humanity as a whole, an undivided organism that
spread across its planetary host?
It created a web that trapped the most.
The slightest touch or tingle on a thread
and you've been seen, heard or you've been read.

This continues now through what time is left to the human race.
Your blood, your DNA, your print, your iris, your face,
you're traced; your thought will be added too,
for all you think will come back to you.

'Computer Karma', it's the modern kind,
no need to wait till the next life, that's blind, it's no more.
Interested parties will knock on your door.
Even if you switch off your phone,
these days now - you're never alone.

That makes it hard to raise your voice,
it's a Global Warming; we don't have a choice.
All we have is a generation left of time.
'Predatory Capitalism' – two words for theft,
theft of a planet and death of a race,
a species extinction at such a fast pace.

Hunger - War - Death

When you're hungry and you've got nothing on your plate
and you're dying and you've lost your mate,
your children are sick because they have nothing good,
and you sell your body or soul just to have some food,
hell is knocking on your door, asking for that little bit more,
life got worse as time dragged on, soon everything will all be gone.

There's a buzzing in the sky,
you don't go outside and you know why,
these days death comes from above.
Those death givers from hell know nothing about starvation or love.
You don't want your kids to be blown apart, dying is not an art. Your children
cry in fear when in the sky that noise they hear, uncontrollable in their
shaking
their fear and sorrow is not their making.
You rage in torment and in silence inside,
you're shaking too; it cannot hide.

You heard the world is warming and all will die one day,
you'd like to have a life, but you've never had a say,
it will take all your effort to just survive today.
The drones have passed; it brings relief from fear,
but only of a kind; in this life death is always near.
You feel desperation and despair for the children sitting there,
who innocently play despite their situation every day.
There is no future that they can behold, except the one just been told.

It gets warmer mostly now, her husband used to say, "the weather is against
us", no water to feed the seeds, and they cost so much to buy, for they do
not regenerate, a year of life, that's their state,
they do not return again, they come with pesticide.
Ironic as it is at the end, for many now, pesticide becomes your deathly
friend…if you're not blown apart.

A Sense of Sadness

I'm a Bear

I'm a bear but you don't care, as you know by now, we all go extinct,
so you are the bear too.
It's just there was something you could do.
We were not given that capacity that humans have,
to think things out, to think ahead,
and plan for the future, which is dead.
I live in the moment, being a bear, we all do,
about time, we don't care.

I'm a bear but you don't really care,
you don't even care about your own,
neither' where your old sleep, nor' where they roam.
So I could be a bear or any other beast out there.
You think that's cute, let's save them, if time suits, well it doesn't,
and you should know, for your scientists told you so.

Shame on you; for you are the 'beast' in our world.
We confirm to nature - you lost your purpose and your way.
You confirm to nothing real in your day.
Cultured and civilized, mmm,
you only wear clothes – that, every animal knows.

Drowning in the Sea of Hell

The Waters of Forgetfulness

Children drowning in the sea; from wars and climate devastation they have to flee, but with no place to really go. The world doesn't really want to know. Their bodies bounce up and down bloated from what, the water or the oil in the ground? For one reason or another, the world heats: for our kids there will be no treats, they will survive in hell for a while or simply die: sooner or later.

It's a global extermination, who's to blame? Who hides this shame? Those who insist on bringing more oil or gas from the deep; they frack and drill for more money to keep. They want more riches as our kids die. The rich will be okay, they'll build air conditioned palaces in the poisoned sky.

They'll watch on a big screen as our children die. And our world dies too. Burn Baby Burn, because there's nowhere to Run Baby Run. And die they will as the rich fly bye.

Media occupies our attention and distracts our cause; so we'll have no time left to change their laws. The climate laws we have are the laws of death. As I write now the ideas of the final summit come. Do you really think the future is one that won't burn?

Media distraction rips out our heart and our attention they try to part - to separate - to overwhelm - to destroy - for them; the news is simply a toy.

Distract the public with things to enjoy. That way they won't know the planet burns for these companies take it in turns. "Social media will keep them employed; they'll be so overwhelmed they won't know they are being toyed."

Who's to blame for this shame? Those that distract and who take money from this game: after all they call this "CHESS" and the aim of the GAME? Keep your riches from the poor, treat humans like manure and leave a planet in a deadly mess.

King Cap the cruel a capitalist king, as his mountain of money rises, he sits on a yacht and sings, 'screw the poor they are manure.' See the world – travel - kill people; this is what happens when you fly. To know what to change you must see what's wrong; it's an attitude gone wrong. When you see the earth of the dying times - there will be only dying rhymes, there will be no future for our kids to behold: if we don't emotionally feel what we're being told.

We need policies to stop the 1% from the planet-piracy of plunder. We live weak and distracted; is it any wonder, with a constructed media that occupies us and steals our power? On the 99%; Hell will fucking shower.

The 'Waters of Forgetfulness' is an ancient idea, but it's something that we should hold near. Those who forget the past are destined to be tied to the mast of repetition. Yes, our children die in the sea, as millions from war and devastation flee. - Out of sight, out of mind. - a race of beings gone self-centred blind.

It was only a tree

It was only a tree, one of many that ceased to be.
Long lived - a thousand years, poisoned by man's fears.
One after another and in their thousands, they were killed.
Man - what a weakness he has, just because he can.
It was only a tree, one of many that ceased to be.

Paris Plummet

Subtitled "Burn Baby Burn" - It's just the same as "Drill Baby Drill"

We waited till the Paris Summit (now renamed as the 'Paris Plummet') was over, till bringing out this third book in our trilogy of Global Warming awareness.

Our "leaders" have now set our world and the one our kids will live in on a "plummeting train" over the ecological cliff. Well, as our title of this book is called "If all the world's a stage – it's on fire", then this "climatic Paris summit" was a tragicomedy, sadly.

Tragic, in the sense that it represented a last real chance of global change and an escape from capitalist predatory influences leading towards some form of human social responsibility. In short, it not only will lead our kids to live in a heating and resource-strapped planet, but a world of increasing resource wars: civilization collapse and ultimately barbarism: before we're frazzled from this place, that, as if in jest, we call, "Mother Earth".

It's a tragedy in which our "leaders" and large corporations are playing their part as if rehearsed to perfection. Well, yes, we all know they get paid very well to do that, so what's new about that? As our countries will become financially destroyed by the new "wonderful" laws that allow major corporations to sue for a multiple of reasons, smaller countries will be ruined and larger ones will eventually not be government run, but corporation run. Well, a continuation of same old, same old, only more so.

Yes, we have been occupied;
they were playing a game, while we the 99%, were begging for a better form of life for us and for our kids. That option is not on their table.

As our world culture has been manipulated to be trivia-social-media based it's embedded with tendencies to accept deep levels of violent inequality, racial or gender, intolerance of religious differences leading to hatred and violence, surveillance and control and acceptance of police state laws and rules: in short, to accept the laws of the differences between the 99% of humanity and the 1%. This leaves the 99% neither time nor energy nor freedom for social unrest or dissent: **WE'VE BEEN OCCUPIED.**

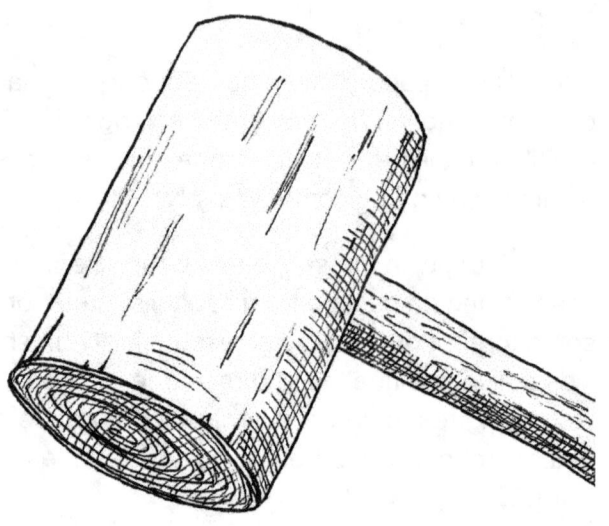

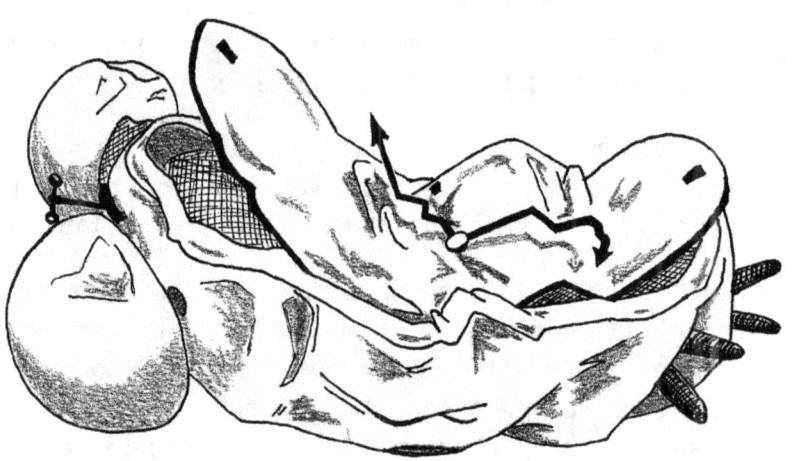

Our hopes and dreams for ourselves and our kids have been subverted and occupied by embedded suggestions from "controllers of might" and power - way beyond our level of resistance.

It seems only a complete revolution of and from humanity will overcome these evil forces which are the "unseen hands" that turn and twist the knife deeper every day, destroying and devastating the already poor and desperate. We are all and will soon become refugees from this corporate and class war on the 99% of humanity, as they turn so called "democracies" into police states of control, while occupying the poor with trivia or survival:

Our "leaders" 'holy-delayed' in Paris and enjoyed the view;
they came up with nothing new.
They continued laws that trash our home.
Our children and theirs will be left to roam.
Yes, that we can our children tell
as they roam across a planet which will BURN LIKE HELL.

BIRDS

At the moment the birds still sing;
but at what point does the heat singe everything?
One day they will stop, before they begin to drop,
like stones falling to the ground.
They'll be no seeds for them to scatter,
and nothing to sing about or chatter.

They die without making a sound.
Other beings will never know why
all begin to suffer and die.
Life goes on until it stops.
The birds in the hot air will fall like rain drops.
They'll give their life up without a sound,
for life goes on until it stops.

The KILLING HEAT

Killing heat drops on your head,
your body sweats, anywhere could be dead.
A world is ravished beyond belief, a planet stolen by a thief.
Disease lies everywhere, it's never far.
Never knowing when you will die,
but it's the only thing for sure, it comes bye.

Death visits everyone you know.
You question why you were born in order to die;
was there a reason for this beginning breath and ending silence? Was a
purpose served at all? It doesn't seem like a holy call.
Some say there is a God; that's hard to believe when the killing heat never
stops; in the killing heat everyone drops.

The Great Egyptian River
De - Nile

Denial: The struggle with the self.
The self that is in denial, 'It`s a Global Warming'.
Do the maths, calculate the paths; it`s not hard to see the reality.
It`s just denial with a smile.
Fossil fuels must stay in the ground below,
"do the maths", it`s not for laughs.
It needs the emotional hit, self-educate.
"Global Warming" is it. 50 years down the line,
it`s gonna be rather HOT, all the time;
a different planet from yours and mine.
The planet Earth will come to be a hot place of misery.
Unrecognizable compared to our day,
science fiction comes our way.

That great Egyptian river 'De-Nile',
where some of us allow ourselves to be taken by
the waters of oblivion for a while,
the ancients called it the 'Waters of Forgetfulness'.

Our attention, taken by inane trivia, distracted away, like a magician would
distract you from the realities of life, taken by new phones, film stars, gossip,
T.V., sleep inducement pastimes, where the rights and responsibilities of
people are being forgotten or eroded by the 'Controllers Of Might'.

I am a particle of all that`s ever been.
I am an atom that you have never seen.
I am your humanity, for which you have no feeling.
I am your conscience, which will send you reeling,
if you were near. But mostly, you do not hear.
I am your soul, which disappears with all the rest.

I am your eyes, to whom you cannot lie.
I am your fate, you have not long to wait.
I am your destiny and it will be fulfilled.
I am your courage and it wants to be heard.

A Sense of Sadness

I am your hope that lies within your heart.
I am your conscience from which you try to part.

The thin circle of organic life that surrounds our "Earth",
extends from just below the ground to the stratosphere
and it contains all that we hold dear.

The hair trigger balance that sustains us
is being sent haywire and losing its ability to maintain us.
There are many things that could be said,
but it's fossil fuels in the main
and this man-made destruction will bring all pain.
And that, my friend, is where we lie
and of course it's where we make our bed,
for together, we will all be dead.

For reasons of denial, human life and more is on trial,
guilty it will be found to be, of 'trashing a Planet' needlessly.
Human and the life of nature will simply die,
but it won't be simple and it won't be painless and there will be no denial at
the outcome of our trial.
Only the angels would be left to watch, but none will cry;
after all, what's there to deny?

$\mathcal{D}$estroying $\mathcal{A}$ll $\mathcal{M}$orality -

$\mathcal{M}$aking $\mathcal{A}$ll $\mathcal{D}$esperate

Should we be 'Dam Mad' – because the reality's really sad? Tears should flow from our eyes at these injustices that the power possessors did start; that this is tragic is no surprise.

How many humans walk the city streets searching in garbage for little treats? The young, the old, the weak, the bold, of course these are times of many but these are still times of plenty. Societies that don't look after the poor are on their way down, that's for sure.

How can your mind be set aright if you have no nourishing food and it's not safe to sleep through the night? 'We don't like to see crazies in the street'; if you have kids that's a fate that you don't want them to meet. Poor kids with those crazy and uncontrolled movements and wild sounding words that they shout, it's no wonder, having to search through garbage to survive another day.

We see the poor and homeless sometimes drunk or drugged – we make the judgment, 'well, money enough for that - go fry up a cat.' Well, if you were in that state and this was your horrendous fate, would you also not want to escape the reality? Just a little something to ease your mind to make you a little blind to your normal every day – would you want to live this way?

Who's to blame for that? We live in a blame culture; so, who's to blame for this society vulture? Who set this beast in motion? Whose policies started to roll the dice? Who leads us, because they're not nice?

It seems our leaders play a game; let's turn our society into one of shame. Let's use the magic mirror trick, because if they see our 'real interests', they'll be sick. Let's blame the poor for their economic woes: that they don't do enough and that's why their life is rough. Let's blame minorities for the troubles of today, that's always good to deflect attention away – from us – from what we do.

Give the common man stuff to occupy their time and lots of causes to hate others; that will help us just fine. Let's give them people to fear, that will hold them glued to us and stick to where we steer – and they will follow like lambs to the slaughter and when they are dead and down, we will have their son or daughter.

We have so many, sometimes we don't know what to do, but they're disposable, this is true. Another war is always good; we trash their education, so joining up they should. The public pay in their taxes for our armies anyhow, so it all works out a treat, that's the common man and their fate to meet.

To die for the greater good and their country to protect, it's a trick we use so much today. You'd think they'd by now suspect the truth – that we have weapons we need to sell and we have revolutions that we must quell. So send the uneducated masses off to war and they don't know what for, that's cool.

"Dam Mad" part two

These are the ills of this Pandora's Box, where people walk the streets; sleep under bridges or under rocks. These are intelligent people that set these policies in action, they've done their maths. 'The poor, they are the sub-traction of our society. They're the surplus we can lose. We have a world to abuse and we're not finished yet.

So we want laws to turn gravity around, we want all the money that's been found and it will continue to travel upwards in space, it comes to us – the 1% of the human race. And all you poor down below, you will struggle, this you know, by now it should be clear, we're on a pirate ship and we're the ones who steer.'

Of course in everyone there's a feeling for the sadness of society, but that gets occupied and distracted by banality. The powerful know this well, it's locked in the deals they sell. When all the money travels upwards in space then we slowly lose the human race.

So, when you see the poor in the streets, old or young, male or female, these days you know that no matter their state, sealed was their fate from policies sent from above, policies not involving common human love. So who's to blame? This is a policy maker shame. These are people who pretend to rule in our name.

> 'Suffer the poor, they should bleed;
> of useless bodies we have a need.'

There's no common goodness, no common care, no sense of humanity that they can share. Common human rights, trashed and shred, yes, this is madness, this is badness, when 'power players' fight for control of planet Earth through all their various methods, it's the devil they serve. You think a God would want a world to be like this? With no care or compassion or homeless and unfed people bombed from the sky, killed in your bed.

No being of care would agree to this madness. But for some, that just leaves them in empty sadness, they say 'There is no God; if there was he would not let this exist, he would not let suffering persist.' But our conception of God comes from our society; so much so, we turn God into an old man with a beard. When you think of God, what image, picture, comes into your mind? What do you find? About all this, are you simply sad or are you DAM MAD?

Goodbye from Mum

Oil - Dark, Silent Death

Dolphins swim and oil drips
from their body it doesn't slide, another oil tanker just died.
A rather lonely death at sea, slowly it began to sink, deep down into the
depths to have a think.
And there it lies among the rest of all that sunk and failed their test. For
some fish life it's a home, from prying foe or eye, but mostly once they're in,
they just die.
Oil is in a place where it's not normally to be found, it's all through the ocean
not deep in the ground, but there it is, silent and dark.
Where it's been it leaves its mark, the mark of death.

Now some powerful people in suits will begin to speak, and with the truth
they will play hide and seek.
'Nature's so vast and big, these things it can take.'
Maybe so, but nature never has a break, from an endless physical assault
upon her being; and the danger that we do, we're not seeing.

We play a role; we play a part, life: 'Hell - that's a dying ART'.
No real 'Art' is ever finished; nature is perfecting her ways.
Inventing stranger things every day, the action goes on until it stops,
which will happen with acid rain drops.
One disaster after another, there will be no time to recover.
But capitalism will have a real good shock, it can use every knock
until we're lying in the ground,
and there's no-one left to make a sound
Goodbye humanity, I am sorry you did not see.

I gave you much to show I live, I was abundant in my supply;
but you did not see, you lived the lie, goodbye.

Love, your Mum, Earth

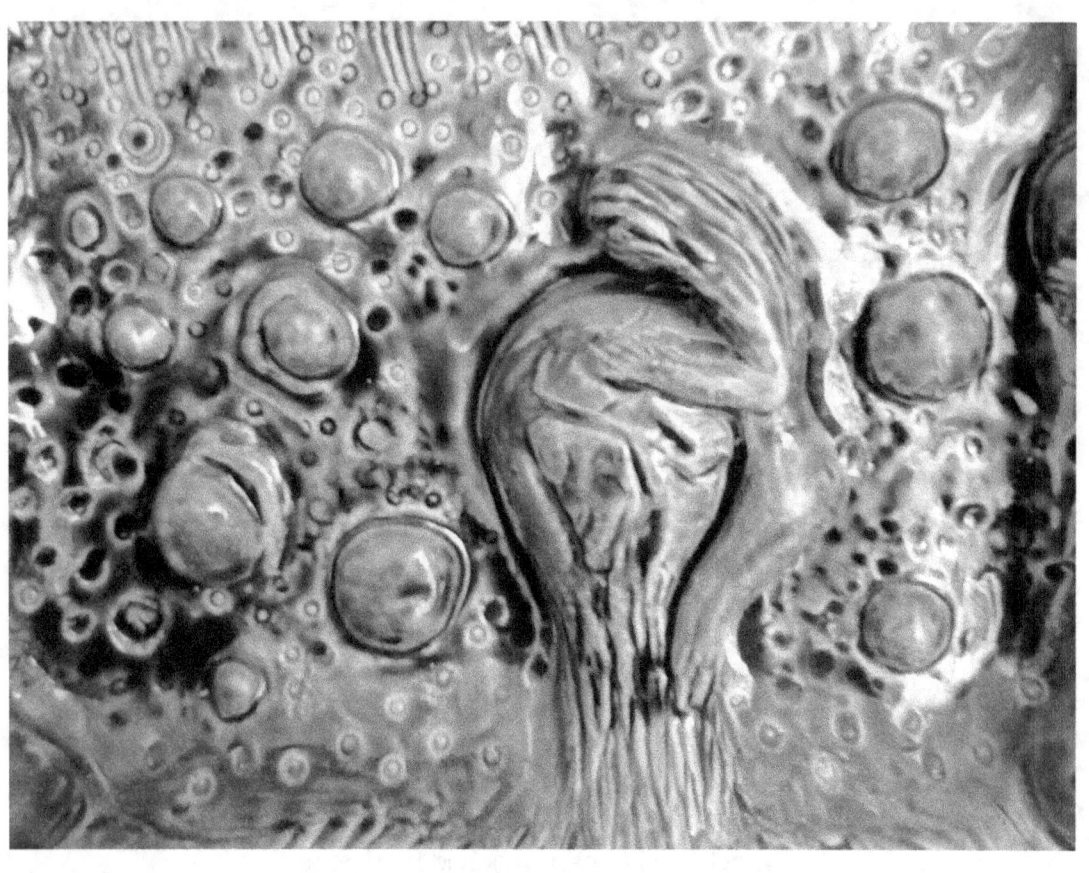

S*ame* O*ld* - *Same old*

Or Seeds of Hope and Survival

Crying in the dark, sleeping in the park

Sometimes quiet the whole night through with only thoughts to trouble you, other times danger comes along. It's the same old, same old song; strangers walking on by, drunk or high.

Needing to exert their power, ain't life a power trip, on this sinking ship we call life?

Too much pressure going over board, but some hope has been stored. In the deep inside I will find it, if it doesn't hide, stored there by my mum and dad, they planted the seeds of hope and survival.

Of love of parents there is no rival.

In your darkest hour it will be there,
it may come anytime - just sitting on a stair - you will be graced to help yourself, it will do wonders for your health, crying in the dark, storming through a park, needing a place to rest your head, the government took your only home and bed. There now are many just like me, oh, how to destroy a society.

'The weather's changing we'd better find a boat.' 'Na it's all used up anything that can float.' 'We'll have to find another park.'
'But they turn the lights out after dark.'

'We'll have to try to creep away.'

'But we're under lock, camera, key, we're all tagged and there's no way out, we leave this place only bagged.'

Countless numbers die every day, there's no way we can stay-strong. Do you think humans got it wrong?

Do you think the rich are where they belong?
Do you think the poor and destitute should sing along?
If so, remember we're just the choir, the requiem is our mire.

As the many try to survive another day just alive,
it makes no difference to the rich,
as to the masses they can live in a ditch.
As long as enough are born to serve,
produce, consume and get ill and die,
they'll continue to promote the lie - that life is getting better,
'Age of Reason', 'Age of Treason', 'Age of Consumerism'
born to consume, fossil fuels to exhume,
burn them for the human cause,
protect them with human laws.
Strange, the human way - anything to survive-
except have an atmosphere in which to live and thrive.
Earth's atmosphere the thickness of a glazed candy apple, when the candy
melts, all the sweetness disappears.

We are the poor and you are the rich,
everything you wear we did stitch.
You worked our fingers to the bone,
now you left us all alone on a burning planet left to roam.
We're the poor and die every day,
you left us no chance or voice to have a say.
Your life, what a way to want to be, and you call this democracy.
What a world you did lead. You cut us deep, you let us bleed,
just like our planet that you do kill,
have you considered the term 'mentally ill'.
"So" - the word used by one of our "leaders", when it was pointed out to him
that polls say the public don't want to go to war. "So"

This is no love poem to God

Born into a world of slavery
whether the end is in the ground from heat
or hanging from a tree,
to make a world of subjects 'being' and then to let them be,
oh, how the people were conned for life and liberty!

What cruel masters rule our world?
Evil has many faces and lurks in many places.
Those who seek the power do not gaze in wonder at a flower,
simply its value on the market in bulk,
neither do they hold it in their sight, nor are they silent in their
night.

Children born, often only live and die a life of pain,
for some, nothing else they knew,
as time they pass through.
For when they're young, time seems eternal;
as we age time begins to rage.
Only if they survive those years, does time raise its ugly head.

 One billion of God's children in the world today go in hunger to
bed. Billions more are born and left unfed,
to live a suffering life and die a poorly death.
As our system continues to turn the heat up on our planet
home, there will be nowhere left for our kids to roam.

With rising seas and much less land and food,
and as we burn, all that once was good,
only one thing will be deeply understood,
that the smiling leaders who with their mouths make much
noise, treated our planet like one of their toys,
and toys is the right word to use,
for these so called 'men' our people and planet did abuse.

Men in years yes, they may well be,
but emotionally inside, boys you can see,
controlled by vanity and conceit,
they led us down a one way street.

Essentially it's 'men's failing,
but none the less there was no real need for this wailing.
Destruction, Death and Despair
there was another path leading to another stair.
The love of the 'self' rules above care for others health
and well-being, this is something now we're always seeing.

It manifests in many a way, it holds the picture you have of
yourself in your mind. You look in the mirror but you're mostly
blind,
only seeing what gives you pleasure or irritates in some silly
way. Vanity and conceit rule this area of your being,
but it's something else you're seeing.

We all suffer from this illusion, the mirror's cracked,
but into our minds complacency there's no intrusion,
it's buffered from the masks that are ingrained within;
some call it a 'holy sin'.

It's work to change this path we take,
for those masks and attitudes never take a break.
It's the picture we present to the world outside,
but from your deeper self this you cannot hide;
moments of sorrow may loosen the mask,
but in general it's 'Herculean' task.

Holy Talk and Mud Cakes

The Holy ones talk of giving thanks to God.
For what, I ask, we've been shod,
cast into a world of need, we have nothing and we bleed,
we're attacked from all sides, death from us never hides.
We are told, believe, you must have faith and trust,
everything that is done, is a must.
God wouldn't have it any other way; he's testing you every day.

This cannot be truly so, I fear he doesn't even know what's going on down
below, in his name. We may be nothing in his eye, as he spits us out with a
deadly cry, survive or die.

But we're attacked from all sides, even nature's against us now,
but yet, we're asked to bow down to a higher hand.
Doesn't God understand?
I have children, I want that they live, every parent wants this so, there's
nothing else for us down here below.

The heavenly stars shine at night,
but they only cover something that isn't right.
There is no justice for this type of life, where it's a world of mostly hunger,
poverty, pain and strife.

The rich seem to have been blessed, they seem to fulfill their quest, they
organize it so the poor stay poor, and die a 'poorly' death,
and they don't seem to care about the poverty and despair.

The despair of ever having food enough, they have magic technology, we
have 'dirt-mud-cakes' to fill our children's belly, just to fill that aching need, to
feel not hungry and not die a seed.

We're not born to a better world; it's worse as the years go by.
The rich are relentless in their pursuit, they have money, food, technology,
but they are mute.

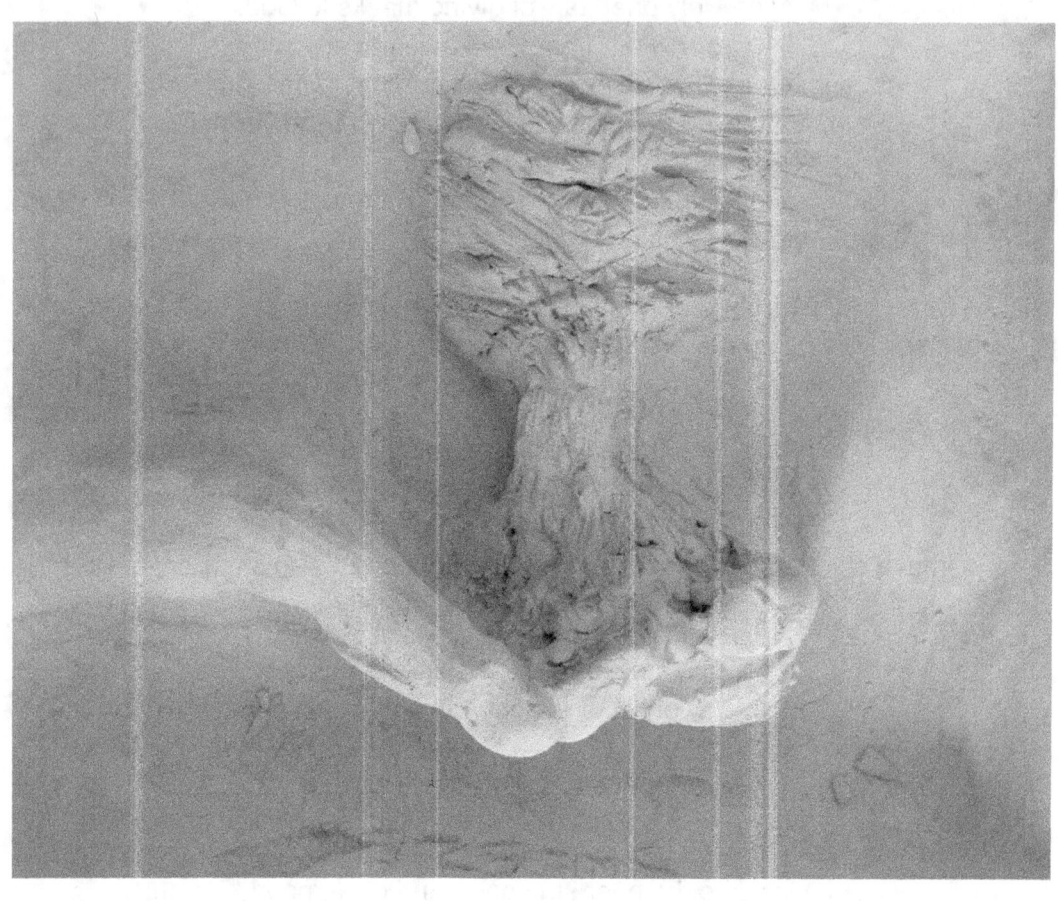

Un-clear Nu-clear

Imagine a world that is no more,
imagine if those in charge could truly soar,
deep into their depth of being,
and perceive what they're not seeing.

Setting laws and rules in place, weaponizing outer space,
what an affront to any God that would be.
A small being - like you or me,
thinking it's all within our grasp,
what an audacity, what a mask,
to allow our weapons to penetrate
closer to heaven's gate.

A hell on Earth has been released;
humanity will be signed off as deceased.
The walking dead we've come to be,
it's just something we don't see.

To take nuclear power and use it to destroy
is just as if it's a boy's new toy.

Being-less leaders are abound, they've got the keys to the house,
they hang around,
working out ways to justify all they do,
they say it's good for me, for you.
Somehow I don't believe them, do you?

What do you think?

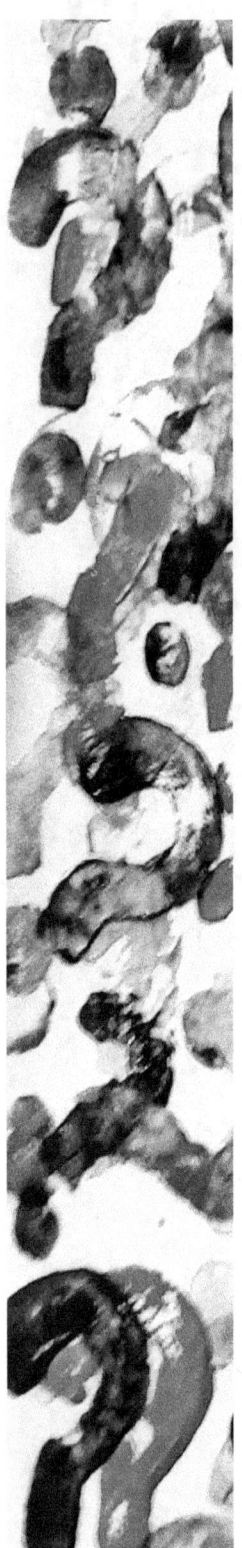

Old words from 'ancients past'
advise us that we need teachers of 'being' at the mast,
teaching us to fulfil the role we were given 'our Earth to till'.
From that, do you think it was the ground that was meant?
That we should dig until we are content,
and burn up everything that we find to a better state of
mind?

Do you think Global Warming is an ALARM?
Do you feel it is right that the 85 richest people in the world
have the same amount of money as the poorest 2.5 billion?

Do you think that those in charge who control the planet
now,   know exactly what they do?
Or do you think they're guessing, just like you?

Do you think Global Warming is unfound?
Do you think oil should stay in the ground?
Do you think politicians ever tell the truth?
Do you think over your head there should be a roof?

Do you feel if something could change it would?
Do you have enough food on your table?
Do you still have a table?

Do you think the rich should be?
Do you think water should be free for all?
Do you think that's a big call?
Do you think people should sleep in the street?
Do you think that's a fate some should meet?

Do you think humans should be free?
Do you think we have no slavery?
Do you feel that's just been rebranded?

Do you think rebranded is the right word?
Do you feel the world is unjust? Do you think that that's a
must?
Do you think the world is getting warmer?
Or do you not believe in all that stuff?

'Teachers of Being', do you think that is what we have?
Do you think our leaders bring a balance?
Do they rise to the occasion?
Do they rise to the need?
Do they our world's population feed?
Feeding the population of a planet is not a big call,
it could so easily be done,
it's within the power of those who think their money is for fun.

Do you think it's true that only 90 corporations control 80 %
of all the fossil fuels? Do you think some play us like fools?
Do you think politicians should be the guardians
and elect of the people?
Do you think austerity measures serve the poor or the rich?
Does it ease the government's financial itch?
Do you think there is anything you can do?
Do you think you would do anything if you could?

Do you think your thoughts should be private?
Do you feel it's right that companies indoctrinate the young?
Do you think you sing that song that they want sung?
Do you feel your emails should be read
while you lie asleep in your bed?
Do you feel it's right that you're tracked wherever you go?
Do you feel freedom and privacy is a human right?
Do you think the really rich should share their wealth?

Would you?

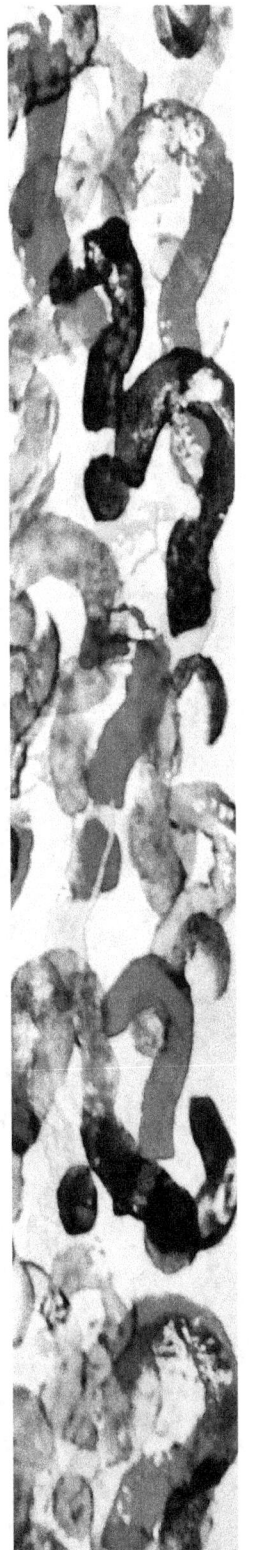

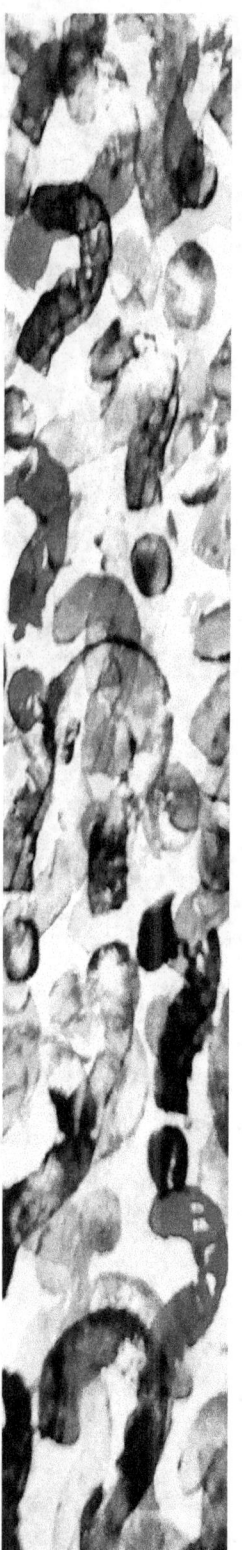

There are needs and there are needs,
and there are warnings that we don't heed.
In our time now our planet's on an edge,
nature's tipping, and it may throw us off the ledge.
If that is done the window of our time will shut,
there's no way back to bring a balance; the rope is cut.
We have a generation at the most
to find leaders of 'being', to be our guide and host,
to lead us back to the balance we must achieve,
so that our only planet, we don't all leave.

Do you think that governments are in planning for future
devastation?
Do you believe that 1,000 species a week become extinct?
Do you believe that half the fish in the ocean are gone
and the rest are on the brink?
Do you think that we will invent technology that will save
us?
Do you feel that's possible within the next 15 years?

Do you think life is meant to be just a party?
Do you think fashion is important?
Do you feel children should be fed?
Do you think other beings have a reason to be bled dry of
security – food – family – life? Or simply have no bed?
How would you feel if it was you or your wife?
Do you feel you have a reason to live?
Do you feel others have as well?
Do you feel people in power should be held to account?
Or do you think they should their money count?
Do you think it might be nice if we had some?

Do our leaders have developed 'being'?
What is it that you are seeing?
Those who only seek the money and the power

will bring rains down upon us and it will not be a shower.
And with those rains the devastations will come,
and it will affect all, we will all succumb.

Do you think people should feel safe in their home?
Or do you feel we should send some a drone?
Do you think we should invade other lands?
Do you think when we do, they should understand?

Do you feel it's right to keep most of the world on
starvation wages?
Do you think we should raise it only in stages?
Do you think the poor should be looked after and fed?
Do you think the homeless should have a bed?

Do you think it's true that most fossil fuels have been put in
the air in the last 25 years?
Do you think we should shed any tears?

Do you think that 2 Billion people should go to bed hungry
every night?
Do you think we should care about their plight?
Do you think things should change?
Do you think it's within our range?
Do you think others should think like you?
Do you think you know just what to do?
Do you think the way you think has been manipulated?
Do you watch regular T.V.?
Do you think you know what you see?
Do you have the latest telephone?
Do you like going to the movies?
Do you feel it's right that governments blocked help to
alleviate climate change?
Do you think that the North Pole is not melting?

Do you think the way you think has been manipulated?
Do you watch regular T.V.?
Do you think you know what you see?

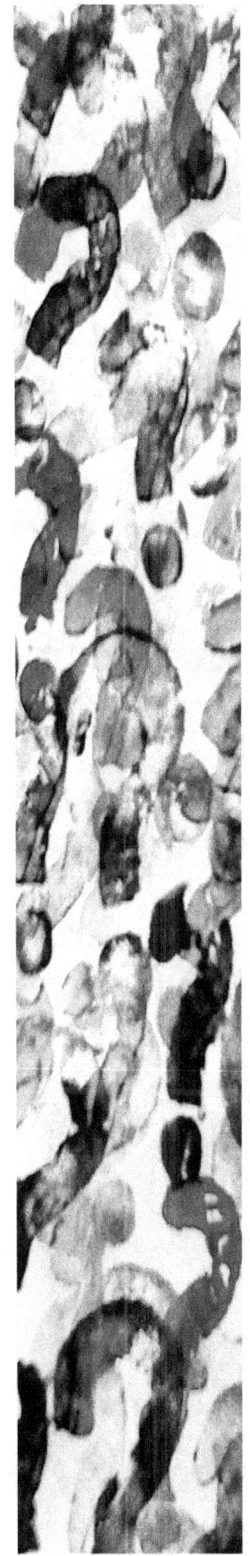

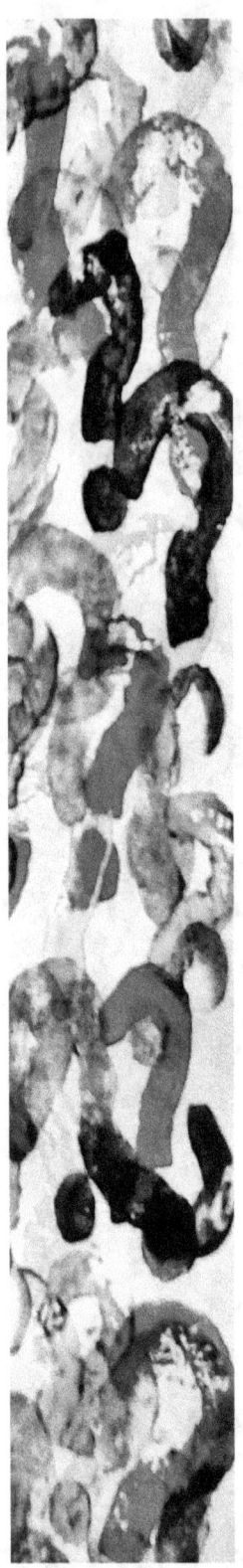

Do you have the latest telephone?
Do you like going to the movies?
Do you feel it's right that governments blocked help to
alleviate climate change? Do you think that the North Pole
is not melting?
Do you think it's too late to care?

Who the hell do we have in charge of our ship?
It's all humanity on this trip;
this isn't about a country, border or land type of thing,
it's about our planet, which for us is everything.
It's all we have and it's all we get;
unfortunately, those in power and control
have us trapped, within the 'net',
and yes, it's growing large and captures most,
but it's not organic, it's a virus in our host,
and like a virus it attacks all cells, it spreads unseen
underground wells, it travels and multiplies itself,
it leads us to being out of balance with our health.

Do you think it's right to continue with the horrors of war
when nobody wants them?
Do you think GOD would agree?
Do you think the majority of the world wants to live in
peace?
Do you think from destroying them we should cease?
Do you think GOD would agree?
Do you think governments should look after its people?
Do you think it should only look after some people?
Do you feel the homeless should be left homeless?
Do you think the hungry should speed up and die?
Do you feel it's right to impose austerity measures?
Do you feel it's right to attack the poor?
Do you feel it's right that they are treated like manure?

Do you think women should be safe to walk in the street?
Do you think violence they should meet?
Do you feel women should be safe in their home?

Do you feel your mother should have that right?

Do you think people of the world need a cause to come together?
Do you think there's a greater cause than Global Warming?
Do you think there's anything you can do?
Do you feel you want to do anything?

So, what do you think: do we need to bring a balance back
to save us from this attack? For it is an attack,
on the human way of life.
Life - normal survival - is hard enough;
we don't need all this extra stuff.
From being-less "leaders" we've been led away from where we should be
today, what do you think? Do you have a voice?
Do you have a say? Do you have a choice?

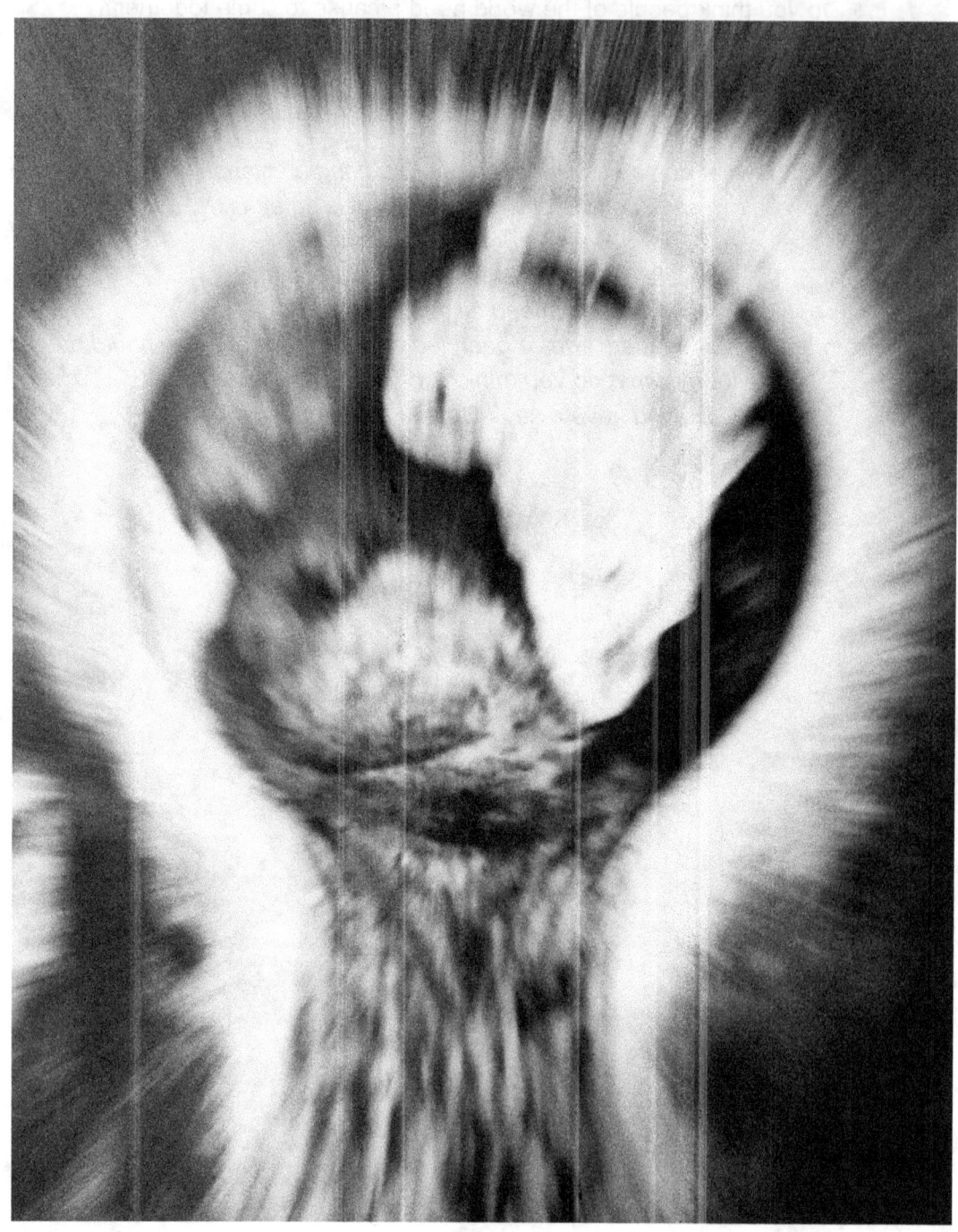

A letter of concern from a passing planetary tourist

Dear Humans, this won't take long, I'm passing at high speed actually and slowing down just long enough to drop off a letter.

It's hard, I know, life: it's hard enough anyway. We lose the course of our own life so easily, so often and to make this effort that is required of you now, seems impossible.

The forces that have led you to where you are now, are powerful; alone, these forces seem insurmountable. It would seem as if there were nothing you can do, I have the deepest sympathy with you. – That familiar saying for many of you, 'you're between a rock and a hard place', is deeply appropriate.

In general, you have come so far over the many centuries that have now passed, against all odds and difficulties; you have realized many things that were wrong and tried to right them.

There are and always will be the misguided, the misdirected, the blind, and the selfish that lack 'Presence of being'. On this aspect of life - humans are not equal.

A lack of being or this personal power of 'presence', its misuse or mis-direction in certain people, has led those people to do things from wrong motives, that have led to wrong and disastrous outcomes. This is not your fault; it is connected with the difficult place or position in the scheme of things that you are in. Sadly, it has affected the general course of your development as a self-evolving species-self, being the important word, and you have been evolving, to a certain extent of course; this has been clear to all who can see. You have that ability to observe yourself, your inner life as well as your outer, if you so choose; the beings you call animals, do not.

But your species is connected to nature, but not only of course. Life, any life, does not come by accident. This many of you realize, which may be conditioned in your culture, time and place you were born into, or it may come from something that lies deep inside you, that manifests as a search for meaning, the meaning for life, in particular, the meaning for your life.

There are many forms of life, of the most basic and visible; you have observed on your planet - and it is your planet - for you humans exist nowhere else, other 'beings' are different. (This, unfortunately is not a compliment.)

There are lower and higher forms of life; you cannot have one without the other; that simply wouldn't make any sense at all. The only question for you would be its visibility or invisibility. You have succeeded in penetrating through the natural barriers that exist, to observe - and interfere with - the lower worlds, a different level of life, the cellular, molecular and electronic worlds. You see connections, interactions and formations, and you, as you know have reached a stage where you can alter their combinations, functions and possibilities in not always desirable ways.

But that is only in the lower direction, fortunately or unfortunately it is harder to see or recognize the other direction. A higher level in the opposite direction is what you call nature; it has its own life span, its own power and its own path of existence to travel and to fulfil. Remember, that life, any life, is not an accident, no matter what you can observe or interfere with in your laboratories, you can only affect but not create life itself. That power is not given or possible for humans to know.

So, nature must try to take care of itself; but, is just as humans and other sentient beings are, contained and connected to nature. Nature itself is contained and obviously connected to the planet. In being part this very thin film of organic life that surrounds Earth, an even higher level of life, which, like all life, must care for its safety and well-being. In much the same way that if your body was ill and had a virus, that was threatening your survival, your body itself would struggle to be well again and bring a balance.

'As above, so below', or as below, so above, it makes not much difference how you look at it. Nature and the planet itself will bring a balance back, but on their time scales, which for them will not be very long at all, but almost unrecognizable for humans.

All this background information is needed to come to the point eventually, but for now. To repeat, that in general, you have done very well - against all odds - you have seen, recognized many things. Your talents and possibilities are not fulfilled as yet, your capacities are still unused, as many of you recognize. Just the simple observation of the capacity of your brain, less than ten percent in use, think if that was one of your computers, only using ten percent of its capacity, what untapped power would be left, and what would it be for, all contained within every little 'human being'. (And yes, you are very little.)

But even with just that ten percent, what you have achieved is momentous. Over the eons of your existence, you have reached a stage where many of you realize the absolute horror and wrong doing of taking the life of other beings, of course, many not yet, but compared to the past; well done. Also to care for others of your tribe, of course that works also on levels, as most 'things' do, your care for family and siblings is inborn, it's pre-set. You can ignore it, but you suffer if you do. Your care for your tribe, your clan, your people, that's necessary for survival over a long period of your time.

Forms of sacrificing life were abundant or transformed; the strong tendencies of the killing and eating of beings similar in existence to your-self for their flesh is also on the decrease, and would continue to do so, if that path had time to develop; unfortunately it does not. Your path now is on another time frame. A bit like the wheel of a bicycle, with many spokes leading to the outside frame, only there is more than one rime of possibilities.

And the latest development of your conscience and consciousness, which is astounding in itself, is your care for other beings in places and other lands, people like you, like your tribe, but another tribe. People with different cultures and different beliefs, different worships and customs, of a different colour and type, your ability to care in general for other beings, that you will never see that are similar, but different. As I'm only passing, I'll skip over a lot of history here.

You were given a great advantage as a race over other sentient beings and other species of your planet. But with a greater gift and possibility comes also a greater responsibility, for as you say, every stick has two ends. You were not called 'homo-sapiens' 'wise man' for nothing; it was an aim to try to live up to, a being who could become a 'guardian' for other beings.

You have a planet with a certain amount of natural laws that you must live under; you know some of them; you formulate them in many ways of expression, from as simple as an apple falling from a tree, to more grander names and phrases, 'You attract the same in response', Karma',

247

'Cause and Effect', the Laws of Physics, etc.

To the point: the Laws of Physics dictate, that you can only burn a certain amount of poisons in your atmosphere before the natural effects of increasing Global Warming appear, killing off life at your level and below; it's a natural effect, it's physics. You cannot change this anymore. But what you do have, even though as you like to say, "The odds are stacked against you", you have the possibility to respond differently, to adapt to necessity. That alone should highlight the untapped powers of your intelligence.

And yes, the odds are highly stacked against you, this is true. Some of your own people, who have come to power and control resources and policy are sadly speeding the way to the destruction of your civilization and general species extinction.

It is no easy path you have, and unfortunately it's the most critical moment of time for all beings of your planet. Your position is not one that any 'aware being from another planet' would consciously seek; you've been led there blinded, misdirected, and hypnotized.

Misdirection and indoctrination comes in many forms, it's difficult to wake up from (the trick of) the illusions of thinking you are making a choice, while you sleep to the reality. Unfortunately, that for Aeons has been the way of control on your planet.

The difference now is 'Speed and Time'; mass distraction and misdirection through your latest communication developments allows everything to be almost instant, devastatingly so.

The indoctrination of many peoples simultaneously has sad and predictable consequences. When you occupy your young with inane trivia and the old and poor with survival, then there is no time, neither energy, nor a cause to wake from this hypnotic trick that casts a very wide 'net'.

So, dear humans, time and circumstance are not on your side. The young of you will continue to be tricked into having the illusions of freedom of choice and in general leading you to self-interest. The old and the poor will continue to be occupied with day to day survival. Those who are a little 'better off' will consider themselves lucky, for a while; they may make a little noise, but in the main they will be silenced, either by the distractions or the deflections of misdirection until there's no time left.

When time for you runs out there is only one scenario available with different 'degrees of disaster'. On one level there will be a complete collapse of your civilisation as your planet heats, eventually beyond liveable conditions. The 'powerful and the rich' may survive a little longer, but in regards to the times scales of nature, the difference is negligible, perhaps a generation or two longer.

There is only one possible 'real hope' for your humanity dear people, of your planet Earth. A world collective action and consciousness for your own survival; as a mainframe, energy extraction from your planet's body must cease, slowing down is good, but cease it must and soon. (In regards to real time – NOW) Many of your 'beings of caring' have solutions, but they are not in positions of power and do not rule your planet. Instead you have leaders with dominating and destructive degenerative tendencies. The people of your planet must be transformed into a global workforce for producing planetary un-harming techniques of energy production.

There's something else for a multiple of reasons; but as I'm only passing, I will keep it short. The horrors of your wars must cease; unlikely, but a necessity. You as a race are now at war with the laws of physics and you're losing, primarily because you have leaders with no 'developed being'. The continuation of your wars fuels the flames of destruction. People don't want war that has always been clear. For you as a race, it has been manipulated through your 'being-less leaders', these are powerful, corrupt, destructive interests and influential forces at work; it's hard to wake and break from that; you have my sympathies.

You need an awareness movement of CARE –

'**C**an **A**lways **R**emember **E**arth'

Yours sincerely and almost with love

A passing planetary tourist

A Sense of Hope

I tell you nothing you do not know

I tell you nothing you do not know - I tell you only where we will go.
Deep in your heart you know this to be true
for when I look in mine, I look in you.
Let's journey for a while together close bye,
it will help, for so much of life pretends to be a lie.
You understand that these words are for you as much as me,
we understand things silently.

Some say there's nothing to be done,
that we all die under a warming sun;
but when you look in you,
you know this is not true.

Our life of many moments, yes, one day, will disappear.
But yet, we often wait on a life that's waiting to be lived, it's near,
if only we could stop taking and simply give.
To live a good life may not be the case,
but to not live a bad one while we're in the human race.
Like all people there's much to what we are blind,
and we do hope that there are other aspects that you find.
You may have some things to say, you may wish to join in some way, for
every human has a different story to tell.

We all have ideas that could lead us to be higher than where we are now;
all it takes is for it to begin somehow,
just to begin to bring a balance, to equalize the scale.
That would help humanity not to fail.
You care as much as we do,
life's a mist, but it's becoming 'see-through'.
There is much you do suspect; and there is much you can detect,
all you have to do is to look, observe and see.
It would be good if you could sense yourself simultaneously.
That would be 'the icing on the cake', take a bite, humanity's at stake.

SOFT - CARE

Saving Our Future Today –

Can Always Remember Earth

It's always nice to keep it short,
all those things that are usually bought.
The world of acronyms is always there, especially today,
but here's the title of this page, soft care – should be all the rage.

Saving Our Future Today – Can Always Remember Earth

CARE: of course is always good,
it's what humans would do if they could,
if they were left to work it out
and were not controlled from the media shout.
And Earth needs a remembering, it's where we tread every day;
we all know this in some way.

Of all the things we can do and we can spend our time,
a little bit of care for Earth would be softly fine,
something needed as we run out of time,
kept by controllers in the dark, 'occupied' to play in the park,
full of amusements and things to buy as our planet starts to fry.

SOFT: Saving Our Future Today: relevant due to the urgency of the
situation, from Global Warming there's no cessation;
but there is a window of opportunity,
it's just the future is misty, never clear enough to see,
but it's there, it can be had,
but it needs a struggle and not to stay in silence and be sad.

A soft revolution in thought:
Why? Because it's the attitude of the old and rich that must no longer be
bought. Revolutions are always repressed in well managed ways,
putting people to the test, many die with much suffering – societies and
cultures destroyed, if those in power they have annoyed.

Organized wars for 100 years mostly politics played on fears.

So a SOFT revolution of thought spread through the world today,
it needs the young to have a say.
Those in lands that are oppressed have no voice,
survival is there only quest, to make it through and survive another day –
understandable. It needs the young of the western world,
who still have a voice not yet curtailed.

Of course, it's weak there is no movement,
in the last ten years there's no real improvement.
Some things are happening here and there;
about divestment from oil stocks, people now care,
it activates the young and old and people to be bold.

It needs a revolution of thought and care for peaceful actions everywhere,
there's so many things you can do, it needs to affect the old, the rich too.
Sure, maybe they'll just care for profit and shares; well, that's what they do,
it's in the system like superglue.

A SOFT revolution of care, affecting everyone, to raise their voice for one
cause, Real Global Warming Laws,
would affect a change in all societies.

Wars could never be allowed. – Isn't that a dream that we would love to be
seen? Politicians would be cowed into submission for the greater good. Ah,
if only they could.

15 years max and you're off the tracks.
So you wanna play around or get off your backs,
stand up to raise your voice,
make a soft care revolution your choice.
Everything can be well managed,
except saving a planet that we have damaged.

Attention will be taken and people will be shaken – down again by well-
chosen media information. You know the situation;
you live it every day; the old, the rich of now will all be dead
by the time real heat hits your head.
So it's 15 years max, just to keep the train on the tracks.

You never know what you can do, even you.
There are so many real people in this world of being-less leaders.
You are the leaders, you are the young;

it's your song that needs to be sung.
Don't be conned anymore by being-less leaders who don't lead,
you need a planet and you have a planet in need.

At no time in the history of the human mystery has it been more important
for people to come together, to have a collective voice;
and at no point has it been more difficult due to bad laws and governing and
multiple surveillance of choice.
And at no point in time will we ever have this slight window of possibility
again, one voice one cause; it needs millions of you,
to be true and to ask yourself, what you can do.

The Writings on the Wall

The writings on the wall: there to see for one and all.
So wherever you may be, feel free to use the media of Graffiti.
Draw the dying, draw the damned, with graffiti it can't be spammed and
remember: a picture says a thousand words;
and an impression all at once, if it penetrates people to the core.

When they have a cause and raise their voice,
then for the brave there'd be no choice.
Use the skill in your ART - drive the nail into the heart.

Make people stop and look in awe;
and they'll remember what they saw.
And in the dark of the night when all things are quiet,
they will look at and they will ponder.
Then perhaps no more moments will they squander,
and in the darkness of this coming night,
they'll remember what they saw, what it was you put upon a wall.

Want Improvement? Join a Movement

You want a choice, raise your voice. If you want change and would like to have a choice in how the world ends, then join a movement if you want improvement. You'll find one that's close and lies in your range.

Your feelings may be vague and be under the illusion that there's nothing you can do; but in the end, to raise your voice is really up to you. It's not about one day, or someday. It's about now – today; it's about people going astray and implementing policies affecting the world over.

In almost every country, in almost every land, there are policies in action that we simply do not understand – where they will lead. But you know them, for some people try to make some noise to wake up others to what destroys - social life and all life on planet Earth.

It's a process that is slow; all social change takes time to grow, but time for change is something that we're losing fast. It's almost passed. Our scientists tell us our future is limited the end of the pendulum swing, time doesn't last – not for us. So you want improvement? While you can, join a movement, be an uncommon man, make a change, take a step, any movement will do, for they must join up for something new.

All demands are inter-connected these days; the financial leaders of our world don't change their ways, they're in control of the speeding train and they're not stopping. There's no refrain – from the policies destroying all life on Earth.

They give you toys to distract you with suffering and lots of media noise, they attract and they distract. So you're dispersed, you have no common state, no common voice, no common cause, multiple movements struggling against multiple laws: keeping the common man separate and apart. It's a society of control sort of thing, it's always been this way. The common men - keep them separate and apart, these days through media, a modern art. Fears and daily struggles, safety, money and food attract the people's attention into the trivia of life; tell them it's for their own good.

From one extreme to another we're kept occupied. It's a word 'they' like; we're too busy struggling and occupying ourselves, our self-hypnotizing drinks been spiked. They don't have to do much at all; we wake a little to the reality of life; they pull a few strings, give us some strife and down we fall back into the swamp of our daily troubles.

It's a really cool trick, seven billion beings all with different seeings; half the world occupied with safety and survival, the other half with inane media trivia that has no rival. Told to party and consume as much as we can, it's the way of the normal man. There is no alternative, this is the rule.

RULE = Regulate Unwanted Lives Everywhere

Control dissent, control their lives, let them marry for that gives us money too. It's a big business with everything involved, but not only, it calms down the mass dissent and interruption of our ways. They won't worry about our corruption in their suffering days.

So that's the story as the story goes, it's rather short but in reality most of it you know. You live this life, it's your choice if you want to have a voice in the ending of the story; it could be yours for the making, yours for the taking, 'if you want improvement, join a movement.' If you're individual and apart, then change, in the time we need it most, becomes a dying Art.

Reminding Poems
from
"Seeds of Sorrow - Seeds of Hope"

Compassion

How can a Hero awaken on such a scale
that would make all other movements by comparison pale?
To awaken to the need, to realize all humans bleed,
that all you see and those to come
will have a warming fate and they will burn.
The pull of barbarism is a powerful force,
for in the end that's where this pull leads of course,
humans slid back down to the savage state;
the house was shut with a lock on the gate.
No way to return, we let our home planet burn.

Probably, only the power of
compassion on a massive scale,
could tame the dragon that does
prevail.
The permanent realization of certain
extinction,
that all our children will die 'the
warming death'.
It seems we need to be taught how to
cultivate compassion;
it might be the antidote to the patient
being ill.
We, of course, are the patient;
for at a certain temperature everything
ceases to be, there is no pill.

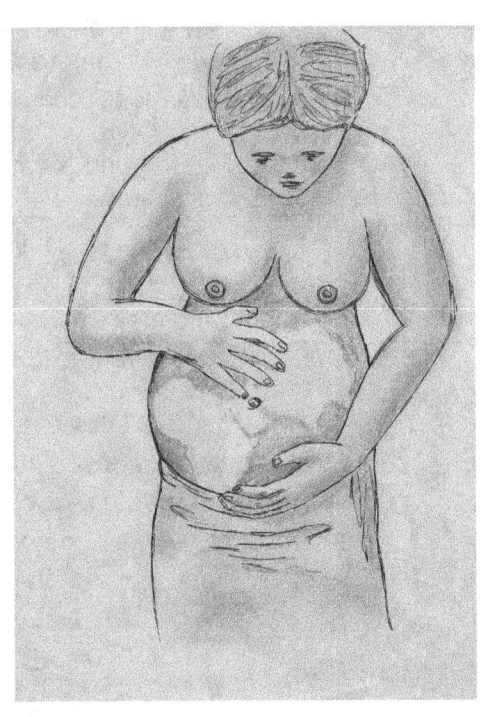

SEED

There are no politicians in our range,
who have the personal power to bring change;
they are weak and they are bought,
and they are not what we sought.
We seek a change; it must be social;
it must be for the common good.
And if all the young could join this cause,
then succeed we would.

There is a movement and it's called SEED
and it will grow with our need,
it stands for Saving Earth Every Day,
there is something you can do, in your own way.

All it needs is for you to become aware,
not just of you, but of everything that is out there.

'They' condition us when we are young,
and 'they' only have one song 'they' want to be sung.
'Join our happy merry little way, buy new things every day;
we'll take your money and your time,
and you'll be so 'occupied', you'll think you're fine.

We'll give you fashion and great things to buy, lots of new stuff to try,
we'll give you a voice and give you a vote,
but we'll stifle it in your throat.
There's no way we'll let you speak,
we'll give you drugs to make you weak, and even them you'll have to buy if
you want to continue to live the lie.

You will think that all is fine, but we really control your mind.
Take all the actions that you like; whatever you drink, we will spike.
We have the greatest media minds in the world in our pay.
Hell, we give them more money every day.
They will place our stuff in your mind; and we even tell you,
because we know you're blind.'

Well now, our eyes are open and our mouths are too,
and we know just what to do.
Become a Hero, take the path,

don't deviate - incur their wrath.
The cause is greater than we know,
our planet's melting down below.

Silence Through Fear

Silence through fear is a common thing. We all suffer from its sting,
it should be forgiven and not held to account,
we are all silent; this we find out.

It's said these days we have a 'culture of conceit',
well yes, but who is the driver in the seat?
The culture of ideas was meant to lead humanity to a question,
could each individual have a clearer perception,
about themselves in their role in the world they live,
is there something more they had to give or become?

We've allowed our society to come to a place, a state, where our children
and we will have an increasingly warmer fate.
This will become clear with passing time;
but it's the 'silence of the good people' that kills something so fine.

The wall of silence, invisible to the eye, is a strong wall, little gets by;
it's a wall that's fed and built with bricks of fear,
it's a wall where there is no humanity near.
Humanity's guilt must be forgiven,
for it's hard to look at oneself and say, 'there is something wrong,
this is not where we belong.'
This is something we hold dear, but we are silent through fear.

Keys, Locks and Chains

What is the right key for change? What's possible, what lies in our range?
What do you think? What do you feel?
Do you believe you are young and should have some fun?
Or do you think there is more meaning to your life?
Can you the 'hero' become
because the older generations did succumb?

Instead, 'they' put the idea in comics and films and manipulated us,
the young, all for profit and all for the same song to be sung.

Carrots on a string: T.V. shows that will make you famous if you can dance,
sing or anything really, break a world record, set a new pace in our modern
society called humans in a consumer race.

They give you 'heroes' for your age;
everybody needs it, it's always the rage,
someone you will try to be like, it's a drink that they spike,
it keeps you subdued and under control.

On T.V. or in films, what film star said a speech,
that kept you in their reach,
to make you feel it's just for you,
oh yes, you could have said that too.

There's a fire outside and it's burning at the door.
'Oh, I heard it all before, yup, 'fire at the door',
of course, it's there to an extent,
but we're ok, honey, make sure you pay the rent.'

Poems from the Future

"Rise of the Heroes"

The Heroes that saved the world from Hell,
the Heroes rose because they had a song to tell,
tales of ancient, tales of old.
We must become Heroes, we must become bold.
It's something that the rich never thought would sell.
Join a movement, do it now, boycott the companies from Hell.

The young Heroes of the world did rise,
they began to open each other's eyes
they no longer toed the line,
realizing their world would no longer be fine.

Together they formed their own sacred band,
and sacred it is, for that is what it is to understand,
that there is more to life than having money, power and control,
and that the rich had sold something that belonged to all,
a planet, that we all need, the rich, they let it bleed.

The Heroes of the modern world were no longer individual
and a p a r t; they made a movement and it did start
to change the tide and roll back the wave
to this one movement and this one cause,
their time and life they gave.
The young became the Heroes,
for planet Earth to save.

An idea did start;
who could do the most for life, for it was not a dying Art?
To wake each other with their call, not one or a few, but all,
a generation left to try, they would do it or they would die.

Movements took place to serve the human race;
they were everywhere inspired, they had a cause.
No more of the rich and their selfish laws,
'all for me and none for you',
the young Heroes sung something new.

Injustices were fought; those who started wars must be brought
to seeing it's not the human way to continue in this modern climate day;
exploitation of the world became the past;
the old ways they shouldn't last.

This is a world of young Heroes all.
We have a voice and a call and our world needs us all.
Our call is soft and one of care, Saving Our Future today -
Can Always Remember Earth - some way.

Heroes they had all become, the story of the sacred young,
for it's where they discovered to be true,
'we can try something new
to rule the world with a 'common sense'
and 'common rights' to dispense.
The rich with their destructive ways should not rule in these days.'

A policy of 'one world' came to pass.
Climate Change was the rallying mast.
The Heroes were mobilized to act,
with each other they made a pact,
'save the world, it's all we've got,
no longer will we be sold or bought,
nor observed in our every move.

The powerful, the rich, they disapprove;
it's their attitude that must improve,
there should be no rich or class in our new days.'

These were the words that were said,
as the balancing laws were made and read.

They did not fight the governments of incipient repression
where the police were heading way out of control,
no; they turned to their mothers and fathers,
who made that army whole
and convinced one and all to turn back
and slow down our planet on its speeding track.

With a generation left to change,
desperate measures were brought in range;
parties in the minorities became the world's majorities.
Women, mothers, daughters, all, fought for a human right,
they brought their baring into the light.
The police, the army, the protectors of the rich and powerful in control, were
turned by family members to become morally whole,
to turn back to the 'human way',
to Save Earth Every Day,
a return of 'Soft Care' kept them there.
This was their need and this was their SEED.
Saving Earth Every Day

The Heroes rose to save the world;
it was the young, no longer were they curtailed
despite the difficulties that were placed in their path;
they raised their voice against this awesome wrath.

The wrath of the rich and powerful, whose weapons were many
and could see inside the young's head;
they could observe their every action for a calling to halt,
their 'being-less leaders' merciless assault,
on the human race at a deadly pace.

The young became the Heroes of ancient past;

they raised their voice eventually at last.

The Heroes came in every land; they had come to understand
that together they could work for change,
in a world of possibilities that was new and strange.

They came to realize that their leaders were dead;
they operated only from their head;
they controlled policy and many laws did make,
they didn't care that all human life was at stake.
Their PR had cancelled the young,
and for every new generation there was a different song to be sung.
But the play was always the same, 'buy our stuff, join our game.'

'You too can rise to the rich,
if you treat anyone and anything like your bitch,
tread upon and do not care about humanity deep in there,
in you deep inside. Don't worry about others if you're okay;
we'll give you a vote, but control what you say.
If we don't like it, we can hear, for to us you're always near.
With the tools of our trade, we can have you slayed.'

The young woke up to the fact they had no choice,
the Heroes began to find their voice.
To work, to change, to wake others to this call,
it needed the participation of one and all.
There was much to be done,
but it was one generation of time left or a burning sun.

The Heroes

That conscience is there, it's just buried deep,
so much piled on top it went to sleep.
It needs a prince to come and kiss to awaken once again,
or a Hero to be your friend.

There's a Hero in us all; you just need to listen to your inner call.
It's in your emotions, it's what you feel.
It's the only Hero that is really real.

You have that Hero in you, it was taught to you when you were young,
this you knew.
You just went to sleep with so much of life to do.
To live, gain experiences, get older and thrive;
but now it needs the Hero in us all if our planet's to survive.

And those Heroes have much work to do.
Some will protest, this is true,
others will with others speak, perhaps it's you.

Some may be a Hero with their songs,
it's a common voice, it has to be, there is no choice.
But you can be the Hero in many a way and you can do it every day. A Hero
with compassion always has something to say.

Perhaps there is no Hero, no Prince nor Princess
in these people anymore,
in which the Goddess of greed and uncaring does possess,
'all for me and none for you',
it's their motto and dragon that the Hero must slay too.
Perhaps in some it could be awakened, that I do not know.
But that Hero is you, are you listening? What will you do?

We have a cause, new world laws;
we have a choice;
we don't have to be silent; we have a voice.
And we must raise it, whether in rage or sorrow,
for now today is tomorrow.
You can Save Earth Every Day Somewhere,
we have a need you are the SEED.
Become a Hero.

Epilogue

The Bone - Fire

Remember - Remember

Something so important, they said it twice

'Remember, Remember, the fifth of November,
the gunpowder treason and plot; I know of no reason why the gunpowder
treason should ever be forgot.'
But there may be something that we forgot.

Guy Fawkes, it seems, rebelled against the government of his time.
The mask is now famous as a revolutionary sign,
representing we are all one and all the same, basically poor and all trapped
within an all-consuming flame,
out of a society that's been 'Austerd' out of anything that is good, tricked out
of homes and sold expensive food.

At that time of year more or less – All Hallows' Eve – there has always been
some form of ritual and cleansing.
The burning of the mask and a fire is an ancient form of mending. Our way
with Gods and laws of old, a special time of the year,
most religions and societies hold it dear.

The ancient Irish had their share of burning fires in the air,
giving thanks and praise to their God Crum,
a barbarous custom deviating from an even more ancient one.
They threw one third of their children on the great Bone-Fires,
to pray and give thanks for future crops to bring.
This 'Bone-Fire' it was always called, for in the morning after the flesh was
burned, bones were all that was left and returned.

To make a mask of some inner task and burn it so it's gone,
was to represent something in oneself that was forlorn,
recognized and relinquished and when burned, vanquished.

The strange deviations that came through time in rituals that were meant to
be fine and contain some special meaning – well sometimes they go off the
track, so there's no way we can work out what we should be feeling.

So now, these days we have a mask that seems to represent the people.
The mask is the same, it's gone collective,
it's a general perspective, but it represents a discontented state,
that shows the common man no longer wants to wait,
and hope that some change will come to their world, which is heading down
a totalitarian path.

So, the mask represents a little hope. It's a cry for help in a
'one voice one cause' sort of way,
where the 'common man' can raise their voice
and resonate together today.

This too, of course, can be deflected and turned around so that any group
can be found to share and wear a mask for their own common ground; it's
kind of rebranded as it goes around.

Real meaning gets taken, turned upside down and shaken,
with nothing real left to see, no real meaning for you or me.
This danger will always be; the only reality is a cause, one that cuts deep
and gnaws you to the core, it's Global Warming at the door.
It's a common understanding that doesn't need rebranding.

This mask shows that the 99 are all one
for we all die under a warming sun.
The poor get chucked out onto the street;
a desperate future awaits to meet,
as money travels against gravity upwards in space.
The politicians have a different mask in their place.
The smiles the same and you can tell, 'all for me and none for you';
it's austerity measures you have to live through.
"We know some of you will fall and die,
we can see your fires burning as we fly by.

The police will protect us if they want to keep their job,
our laws give them lots of power over you, the mob.
So yes, protest and wear your mask, demonstrate en masse;
we think you're poor and rather crass.
We fixed it in your education; so you can't really think beyond your station,
we've occupied you in so many different ways; you're busy with trivia or
survival in every one of your days.

Enjoy the fire that you light; it's entertainment on a dark night. Occupied,
yes, we love it that you call it so; it makes you think you're doing something
way down below. But remember that in your pocket you have a phone, so
we will never leave you really all alone.

We will track and disband all your leaders in every land.
You call us the robber barons of the past,
well, that was then and this is now. We control the media, the governments,
the banks, the police, the army.
Do you really think you have a say?
We have modern psychologists to help us in our pay,
and pay them well, that we do,
for we took all your money away from you,
you who dare to wear a mask,
and think you'll get some back just because you ask.
That's a 'Herculean' task.

'Remember, Remember', a word so important they said it twice,
and because we distract and occupy you with trivia, survival, and austerity,
you forgot to remember we've done this before; we're not nice. Well, now it
continues till the water's at your door.
If you still have one by the time, we finish with what we take.
So keep your fire burning for it's you we may burn tied to the stake.
Someone has to pay for spoiling our day; and if you all continue to wear that
mask, we'll burn you all; that's our task."

If all the world's a stage, then the actors and the audience should feel sorrow and rage and it should lead them to understand, that our world unveils as a barren land.

The unveiling of the world to be, depends upon the 99 and what we sense and see. When civilizations start to collapse, for Barbarism, there will be no maps.

If 'all the world's a stage', it's on fire

Then we shall end at the beginning

And if all plays must come to an end;
we'll leave you with a poem that perhaps you can amend.

Those words by the world's most famous bard,
are well known, but it was hard,
for probably 'To be or not to be'
are the words that cut through you and cut through me.
That signifies whether I am or I am not,
which leads us to the most essential question
that in the end all must ask, who am I?

The struggle for the wish to be is much the same for you or me.
Many of us of course never come to that place
where we question reality, the one that hits you in the face.

'To be or not to be', it seems to be a choice, to give your inner life a voice,
the one that's been silenced as the years go by,
that voice that makes the question, who am I?
What is my role, what part do I play, what is it I have to say?
Who am I?

II

When you are sitting and on your own and there is no mask to hold, only
yourself to behold, which is what all writers of ancient past have said, then
that voice can be heard.
It simply whispers in your ear, it's a gentle thing and it is near,
for no man can tell you your role; there is no direction for you to go.

When you sit and become aware and sense, all the multitude of thoughts
and voices that pass through your head,
give you many reasons for saying the words that shall be said,
and they will justify all your actions until you're dead.

But when you're on your own and you're quiet and there's no action to be
done, the mask is off and you come closer to who you are.

That door is not wide open, it's just ajar,
for it needs you to become 'aware' of the things going on in there.

III

Apparently each man must play his part;
for many, it was written at the start.
Their role was given fixed in time, and they must play it to be fine;
but for other actors on that stage of life,
the roles neither fixed nor super glued,
it's a role that can be reviewed.
It may lead to a role of strife, no matter who you may be;
there is a role that was meant for thee,

There is a life 'waiting to be lived',
it has action that only you can give.

Most have a conscience that seems to speak;
it's quiet, it plays hide and seek,
but it nags, pushes or guides us to stay onto a path,
and if we fail to listen, well there may be an aftermath.
We each must pay that price, and that cost it will from us extract;
it's not that we ran away, we simply turned our back.

We became immersed in the other role; the one we play every day,
the one that says: 'I know, let me have my say'.

This is the role that does not question 'to be or not to be',
this role is played unconsciously.
No real conscience will touch this actor's heart,
and from his role he will never part.
But we all fail sometimes here,
we ignore the voice that gently whispers in our ear.

These poems, these words are not instructions on how to be,
they're simply a reminding call,
for we need a lot of help in order to see.
No-one can tell you what to do;
only your conscience can see you through.

IV

If 'all the worlds a stage', well yes, then it's been stage managed,

In this play of human life certain actors cause us strife.
It's not that they play their role bad,
it's just that it's the only role in history they've ever had.
By those who have their roles well-healed,
humanity's fate seems to have been sealed,
and for what and how they do, others must pay.
There is an ending that now awaits us all,
but most of you reading will be dead
before that axe on humanity does fall.

So, in the meantime we are distracted with what the main players say and
do, for they cause us pain, me and you.

Their 'being-less' actions kill many and cause much suffering and pain.
And for much of our cast, the 'walk on extras' of life-
it seems as if we are simply bred for this strife.

Every so often, but with a regular beat, comes walking across the stage, a
man with a treat; he holds a placard, it isn't sweet,
but takes the attention of the audience away, from all the other actions in the
play. And the words there to be read, they always penetrate into your heart
or head.

They 'occupy' you; your attention's been bought,
for that is what it is, the man with the placard sought.
His job is very stable; all it says is 'all options are on the table'.

V

Isn't this an insult and an amazing thing to say,
to threaten to obliterate you in every fucking way,
to blow your world a p a r t
and cause suffering, rip out and burn your heart?

To burn the skin and the flesh, to penetrate into your very being, what is it
that man's not seeing?
From which part of his 'humanity' is he fleeing?

No one can escape, or run away from that threat.
All it takes is for a 'being-less' leader to sweat,

and then millions will die and suffer pain;
it will be instant with nothing to gain.
If 'all the world is a stage' it will be blown a p a r t,
with countless and needless suffering – life – a dying Art.

Where do we get these actors from, who, truth be told, seem to be where
they belong? It's just a question we should ask,
where did they get that horrible mask?

Can they be taken off the stage? Do you hear the audience rage?
There are no spectators of this play, for we must live this every day.
This is an onslaught and offensive to the human way.
Their acting is good but horrific;
and they have a role, it's quite specific.

Sweet words they utter, they sooth the ear,
of those who only partially hear,
keep the audience filled with popcorn and soft drinks.

Then they never know what they 'thinks',
they'll think they will have been well fed,
but it's a lack of real nourishment, only popcorn for their head,
and if the audience do perceive who it is these actors be,
'we'll allocate a small slice of pie, just a bit until they die,
for the chief roles upon the stage of life have been taken,
and the roles of all others will be forsaken.'

VI

'Our roles are fixed, we lead and you cannot touch,
no matter what you do, no matter how much,
we will rock the house and pull the curtain (of life) down,
we will let you know we have been around,
we know just what to do, for we have a saying,
'All for us and none for you'.

'You will never enjoy what we do,
you gave us the power and we control everything except your soul,
but we tell you that even that will be ok,
if you simply do what we say.

We have so much on our side,
there's nowhere to go, nowhere to hide.
You can make a little noise, but we give you lots of new toys
that 'occupy' you in the main,
that take your attention away from our deadly game.
In this play of life we have a plot,
but we supply the gunpowder that you have bought.
So, you little people think you have a voice,
but in reality we leave you with no choice.
You will kneel and you will bow; we control it all anyhow,
we've got lots of pots/plots that are cooking,
we distract you like magicians – where you're looking.'

VII

A play within a play - we can confuse you every day,
we change the background of the scene and set,
give a few more actors, we give and we get.
If we think you understand and begin to see,
we just rewrite, we have scriptwriters working unceasingly.

We pay them well for their thought
because it's with your money they've been bought.
We just tell them what to say and they rewrite it in their way,
words that seem sweet but would really make you sick,
if you could see behind the veil of our trick.

Of course, some of you wake up from the stupor that we impose upon you.
But we keep you occupied with something else to do.
We keep you poor with just enough to live.
We make you worried that no more we will give.
If you raise your voice and put your hand out for a little more,
well, we know where you live and everything you say and do
and we've got lots of people; they're paid by you,
we have the power, we have control.
You have nothing but your soul,
if that.

VIII

So yes, now the planet heats,
of course we know, but it gives us treats.
We're in a system and it's fixed; there's no way to change our tricks, even
we ourselves cannot escape this 'net',
that captures 'everything' and so to a heating end it will bring
this play of life that we have led.
We drained our planet, we made our bed,
for you are the audience and the actors too;
we direct, we tell you what to do,
we get a better rate of pay and it goes up almost every day.
So yes, all the world is our stage and yes, it's on fire.
When you turn the page – of history – you could if you were here, but you
won't be, no-one will; we burned the house down.

And if 'All the world is a stage' and we are bit actors in it,
then you have played your little part
and from your taxes you did depart.
We have them now, thanks a lot, we took all that we got,
we have a rule, we have a creed; all you have we really need,
'all for us and none for you'.
Let's use that bard's other words to be true,
'To be or not to be',
which can be the realization that I am or I am not,
for all you have, we have sold and you have bought.
It was a show, but that you knew; we just kept you 'occupied'.

We enjoyed it, did you?

Endings and Beginnings

*Capitalism or the 'Age of Change' - It's a MAD world –Poor and Destitute
and our kids sent off to wars - Planet Art – Rich – Poor – Spaced out and
Disconnected - Wishing - The Prince -The Sleeper -The Wish - The Hero*

How to end this book, when the aim is to begin something, which has in
essence begun already, an awareness of a global and local need? For
actions and reforms on many levels we need to combat the incredible forces
holding us like super glue to a path that will be devastation for all our kids.

We'd love to be able to offer and suggest the most amazing solution
for stopping anthropogenic induced fossil fuel Global Warming on page 99
of this book, but we don't have one. Some of you do though. In some of
these pages we mention a few options that others have put forward. The
most obvious being: leaving what's left of the oil in the ground and refrain
from using coal, gas and fracking technologies. Many people work for those
changes and that's great.

A massive convert to wind, solar or any sensible alternatives would
be helpful; in turning our financially ravaged and austerity induced
unemployed population into a massive planetary workforce for saving and
adapting to our 'new and coming soon at a cinema near you' 'end of world
scenarios'.

We can still hope, we have a generation left to hope, because till
now, there is no real change. All there is left is hope; but it must be bold.
Change, it seems, got bought up by the rich and powerful.

Hope of course can be bought, used and manipulated and just as
easily turned into another commodity, repackaged, rebranded by the
masters of policy and their 'Goddess of Propaganda called PR'.

The road is long and most definitely uphill. But there isn't a lot of time
left to get where we need to be; this is one of the real situations in life where
- time counts.

As it's unlikely we will write anything like this again, not being experts on Global Warming, simply concerned people and each one of us has their own story to continue and finish, we can only hope that a part of your story will become a part of our story - this story.

The story of efforts in raising a global awareness in regards to Global Warming and all its connected causes, an effort strong enough to bring a resistance to help counter the destructive actions which were set in motion long ago, without thought to the consequences now beginning to devastate our planet, wouldn't it be nice, to have an alternative ending? In essence, to bring a balance to our societies and in doing so, our planet.

Capitalism or the 'Age of Change'

You will have read and understood in some of the previous pages the information that we drew from various sources, regarding the observation that many of the problems in our societies stem from the capitalist financial system most of the world is under and the urgent need for recognition and change from this Pandora's Box of ills that has been unleashed on all of our societies, in one way or another.

All social reforms through history have taken time to develop and gain strength, but this time now is the most urgent that we could possibly imagine. We need a movement to be on the constructive side and work against these connected social, financial and human injustices, which as a side effect, cause and will continue with social and world devastation.

The information that we write about has been reported in many studies on the subject, some by inter-government panels, many scientists of merit and political, social and environmental commentators and plain old simple humans who care: their conclusions and suggestions drawn from their understandings. We quote none of it directly; we just rhyme it, hopefully without changing or losing any of the meaning.

The information changes and updates with every new study that is published along with new assessments of the situation, which unfortunately became increasingly grimmer with each publication over the last 15 years.

Many of you will be aware of or suspect what is happening in our world; but often we avert our eyes and occupy ourselves with the busyness of life rather than face a threat so large, one that we feel unprepared for and so utterly helpless against, which quite frankly, is understandable. It's the ultimate Hollywood disaster movie, only we all have and share the starring role.

It seems, 'HOT' ending guaranteed, *it's just that if the worst of things can be a little mitigated, slowed down, within the time available of about 10 years that experts tell us we have left, then our children and theirs may have a bit longer; then who knows what can happen.*

It's a MAD world

'MAD' is the standard acronym for "Mutually Assured Destruction" in regards to nuclear war. But as we release into our atmosphere the equivalent of 400,000 litres of CO_2 every day, MAD may just seem to any reasonable thinking, appropriate: Humans - Mad - And - Dangerous.

It's rather sad that anyone should even feel that they have to write to bring awareness to this subject. It should be on everybody's lips, it should be in every newspaper. Prominent public figures (should speak every day), religious leaders (in every sermon), politicians (simply stop lying, that would help), media stars (some do try, this is thankfully true), heads of countries (only the poor and not the powerful). International organizations (any would really help), professors and teachers in schools, people who have a voice, people who are listened to should be speaking up loud and clear.

Well, if you didn't fall into any of the previous categories, that now brings us to you and me, who could be speaking up or at least speaking to others. The famous quote from Martin Luther King seems unfortunately deeply appropriate. It's not the one about the apple tree, just in case you're wondering.

The fact that it's not on front page news is cause enough for a book like this. So many others are struggling to bring awareness to people of the world at large in many ways. That alone should indicate the amount of money and effort over the last ten years gone into distraction and misdirection of information, being financed from those who will financially profit through media manipulation of public opinion in regards to Global Warming.

We have a planet that's warming and scientists predicting

devastating outcomes for all forms of life. That famous 'table', of which all options are usually on, unfortunately seems to have no space left for this topic. Well, obviously, it's the ultimate topic, so why not?

If governments could feel shame (God, if only) due to their inadequacy of efforts, over this planetary crisis, that would help: but of course, that will not happen. People should be freer to be informed; and you need informed people to take involved action. Therefore it really doesn't help that the people of the world are being placed increasingly under surveillance and suffer from fear of attack from their own governments if they step out of line through protest or any form of dissent. A ceasing of surveillance of the peoples of the world is needed in order allow them to work together to build movements of action in their struggle against the powerful forces that drive our planet over the edge.

Policy makers and those who work for them, lull us into a false sense of security that keeps us quiet while the burglars are stealing the valuables of the house, setting it on fire as they go. Of course, we tell our kids, things will be okay; we're safe, and if anything is going to happen, it won't be today. As adults, we know the approaching horror and, soon enough, it will be in their face.

It seems on a planetary time scale our window of opportunity is the blink of an eye. So, blink and you'll miss it.

In a study published in 2015 it was found that if nothing is done to slow down climate change, then 'by the end of this century temperatures in many places in the middle east *"are likely to approach and exceed"* the levels that human beings can survive', which obviously means, before that time there will be much suffering and mass migration: hundreds of millions of people on the move.

The poor and destitute – and our kids, sent off to wars

The difficult part in writing this was in imagining the living conditions of people 'surviving' in total poverty, as between two and four billion of our brothers and sisters of our human family do, combined with the living or dying situation of those poor souls that are in war-torn areas. Many are now at the beginning time of mass exodus of devastated people fleeing their homelands to become 'refugees' in a world where governments in the main ignore their cries. To imagine their horror, I simply could not do it justice enough, my apologies. This level of living hell, one would have to live through to truly empathize.

This apology also extends to the poor kids trained as warriors that are sent off to needless wars, over what, oil, or any other vital interest? These kids are taught how to kill, when they are still in the early part of their life education and have been emotionally manipulated through 'behavioural conditioning'. An economy organized so that joining into war becomes an almost only option, for the poor of our society is a – shame. That should weigh heavily on those in power and control, which set and keep this system in motion: unfortunately it doesn't seem to.

There is so much that we do not understand about all the complexities that will occur: which means we will not have covered everything, due either to lack of knowledge or understanding or just the plain simple fact that there's a lot to cover in this very dramatic important planetary crisis, which will soon alter our world for the worse and will most definitely bring the beach closer to your door.

Art - Life

I once read that 'The original purpose of the artistic ability was to transmit ancient wisdom to remote posterity. Well, this is no ancient wisdom, its common sense, a sense that should be common to all. If nothing is done to slow down the heating tendency there may be no possibility of a 'remote posterity' due to the no small detail of 'real time' running out.

We are a species of artists, no doubt about that. We seek perfection at something or many things on many levels, perhaps for reasons we do not understand or even perceive; but it's in there, deep inside, this longing to be if not perfect, then *good at something, good for something*. We are rewarded (that may be only by our ego sometimes, of course) by having meaning, in living a life that is meaningful. People have a deep magnetic emotional wish to feel needed, wanted and useful, we all do; it's inherent in our nature.

If time, money and circumstance allowed we would take this desire and need to perfect ourselves into many other fields of action. The office worker who becomes the painter, the brick layer who not only likes to make an art of building a wall, but of cooking the evening meal, the angry man who wants to be the meditating monk; we're torn within ourselves, due perhaps to many reasons beyond our understanding or control.

You will recognize yourself there, somewhere with your story, for everybody has a story and every story is a mystery. It's the mystery of the unfolding of your life, it's just different for each person and each story has a different ending. Some stories are unfinished or unfulfilled; some wait for the right time...some have no time...and are just short stories.

But to skip a few pages in this story, for humanity, our time is now. There is no choice; we need a voice, saving our planet Earth must become our Art.

Rich - Poor

We cannot expect people struggling to earn a dollar a day, under slave conditions to do much other than survive, due in most part to years of selfishness, uncaring and 'un-thoughtful actions' by the more powerful countries through domination, which have affected the living conditions of the poorer peoples around all of our world. And it is our world, not theirs, regardless of what "they" think.

People involved in different projects are trying to raise the awareness of all people and to affect and inspire as many as possible to resist the incredible powerful and sometimes plain evil forces that have been and still are at work to treat life on Earth and the Earth itself as an 'externality'. The people - and it is people - who control and influence policy on the level of financial value, sadly place their profit higher than the planet and all of the species on it.

There is a tipping point; we're on it and there's no going back. No technology in the world will save our planet from the cumulative interactive effects on the varied systems that allow our planet to be liveable for life as we know it. That all changes!

As the majority of CO_2 released into our atmosphere has been within the last 25 years, then we are responsible. Awareness of the situation raises the stakes of collective responsibility. Sorry to inform you, but, it's not only the largest corporations in the world, sure, they are still inducing the problem and hindering the help so desperately needed to work against Climate Change. But so do we, when we turn our back and sit and watch T.V. and hope for change. It's pretty clear by now, it's not coming. People in power and those who work for them, don't happily give it away; it needs a struggle, a voice, a cause.

Spaced out and Disconnected

To return again to a point that needs repeating: It's hard to consider this problem, its enormity, it's out of our 'reach-ness', especially when it's been organized throughout the world that people must fight just to exist. They must be concerned with day to day survival, never mind the heating planet, the storms, the floods, the heat waves and the other dramatic climate devastations ravaging all over our world. These are local problems, but stemming from global, so they're spaced out, they're separated, disconnected. And that's only in some places, in others there's only mild fluctuations in the weather.

Unless you're affected, there's no personal emotional hit. So, getting through the day, finding work, putting food on the table for your family, takes our energy and concern. Then the enormity of the problem becomes out of reach. Essentially our problem is the same and the people (and it is people) causing it, are the same people controlling global policies and those who work for them, as the governments of our countries seem to do, in caring for companies interests over people. In allowing themselves to be bought and sold, they have unfortunately, to put it mildly, sold humanity, us, our children and the following generations, down the drain, wiping out the majority of all other species on the planet on the way.

One Voice - One Cause - One Art - from Global Warming to Depart

Wishing

Humans by their very nature are a creative and pro-active race of beings. We are not under-achievers, as well as our ability to read, think about and understand, or even misunderstand these words; we have that power of imaginative thought and that ability and power to wish. We can wish for things to be better. Not that we always succeed with what we wish for, but without wishing for something, it will never happen.

We possess another possibility of wishing for wrong things, things that hinder our development as a human or a species. We can be led by selfish desires, but we can also be led by a common desire, a common wish, a 'common sense', a sense based on an understanding that is common to us all, for our common need.

We can imagine a better world even if we never get to it. We can have a collective aim, a collective wish, a collective voice. That may take some time in coming, as we are a disconnected planet. Despite our technological possibilities, we seem to live a disconnected life. Of course, we are maintained that way, 'let's be clear', it benefits the minority to keep the majority dis-connected – self-concerned - concerned with self-interests on different levels.

Only a collective aim, a wish, now - at this stage of our shortening history - will be able to bring us together and back to a balance. Unfortunately, there are so many hurdles and blocks put in place to stop that from happening.

The Prince - The Sleeper - The Wish - The Hero

Nothing comes without first the wish; one has to see what's wrong to wish to change it. This is our fairy-tale and we have a wish, unfortunately only one.

You, dear reader, are the Prince that comes and awakens the Sleeper in the tower, but not only: you are that Sleeper in the tower, as much as you may not wish to be, you/we are in that double position. You have that problem and you have to awaken that power. It is simply inherent; it lies within waiting to be developed. And for humanity this may well be the ultimate labour. You are Hercules, whether you wish to be or not. And like all Heroes you can turn your back and look the other way, but one day we must look in that mirror of the self. This seems like an appropriate time, can't think of a better one.

One day, we must finish the book of our life. Not all endings are happy, but we can wish, let's not have an empty one; it needs the power not only of an individual but a collective wish, one that may be heard in the heavens, one that says, humans want to survive in this vast, beautiful, often cruel and unfathomable cosmos.

The root of the word education is edu: meaning to draw out off, as in water from a well, not to stuff in, as in useless information. You essentially educate yourself, we all do. What we wish to 'draw' out of you, to activate a little, for want of a better word, is that spark of humanity that lies within you, me, in everybody. It's incipient, it's in-born, it's in all of us, whether you're a candlestick maker, a baker, a mother, a company owner, a politician, a thief, a painter, a boxer, a soldier, whether you're homeless, drunk, needy or full of life or rich financially. It can be drawn out, but only you can do that.

We write because we have the normal concerns that most do. One strong reason is that we want our kids to live on a planet that is liveable, and their kids as well, and quite frankly we don't know what else to do. We - like you, like most people struggling in life, to educate the kids, want for their health and well-being, and are frightened and horrified at the prospects of the dramatic climate and social future heading towards us like a 'speeding train'.

On a planet that's heating up quicker than it should be, combined with losing any gains and freedoms on a social level that have been achieved in the last hundred years, and human development over thousands of years, then pretty soon our human history reaches its final chapter if nothing is done. The picture isn't complicated to see, it's just our vision has been misdirected.

To us, to our perceptions, it doesn't seem that quick, but on an evolutionary scale, for nature, it is hours, for the planet itself it's more likely minutes. So time is essential; we have one generation of - our time - left to make a difference, to awaken to the reality of seeing and finding the common cause, the common need and wish, to awaken that sleeper that lies within all of us. You must in your own way awaken and become a Hero, we need a world of Heroes and we need them now.

Okay, dear reader, that's enough of the doom and gloom. We'll end this with a few words from the back cover of our first book in this trilogy, called 'Global Warming – Time Stories'.

'There is hope, but it must be bold, a hope that will empower and enable us to confront the seen and unseen difficulties that lie ahead.

All over the world people dream, wish and hope for a new future, with new possibilities for a real human race. Those seeds are sown, they've taken root already, but now, unfortunately, 'Time' overtakes us, so we are in need of a mass cultivation of seeds of hope, everywhere, in many directions simultaneously for this story to continue, the Human story. We know our story is not over yet, but we are the last generation that can still do something for the future of our children and humanity.

There's a Hero that lies in you,
it's been there since you were young; this you knew.
It whispers gently in your ear,
sometimes this you will hear.
You can turn your back and look away
but sometime tomorrow must become today.'

Epilogue

www.ingramcontent.com/pod-product-compliance
Lightning Source LLC
Chambersburg PA
CBHW081344280526

45788CB00009B/2763